BEATING
THE
IMPOSSIBLE

A LIFE OF COMEBACKS,
EXTREME SPORTS
AND PTSD

DON SCHWARTZ

 FriesenPress

One Printers Way
Altona, MB R0G 0B0
Canada

www.friesenpress.com

The events in the book are all from memory and discussions with friends, family and fellow competitors. Any mistakes or errors on dates and details are not intentional. While we all experience the same event, we may all remember it differently.

Edited by Bronwyn Preece and Lee Schwartz

ISBN
978-1-03-913573-4 (Hardcover)
978-1-03-913572-7 (Paperback)
978-1-03-913574-1 (eBook)

1. Biography & Autobiography, Sports

Distributed to the trade by The Ingram Book Company

TABLE OF CONTENTS

INTRODUCTION

HAVE YOU EVER HIT ROCK BOTTOM? HAVE YOU EVER FOUND yourself on death's doorstep, wondering if you will survive... physically, mentally, or spiritually?

My life has slammed me to the bottom more times than I could have ever imagined. I am still here, slightly bent, bruised, and scarred, but nevertheless here—thriving and smiling.

From the time I could walk, my mom put skis on my feet and my dad gave me skates and a hockey stick. I grew up hiking in the summer and ski racing during the winter, with my family in Canada's Rocky Mountains. An athletic and active youth would be an understatement for how I was raised in Calgary, Alberta. Living life full throttle was normal for me.

At fourteen, I discovered snowboarding and began competing immediately. At eighteen, I won the North American Snowboard Championships. I then moved to Whistler, British Columbia, to pursue a career in the snow.

Back then, I enjoyed sitting on the top of the world and living the best dream life that I could imagine. To outsiders, it must have seemed too good to be true. It wasn't. What appeared to be easy success came with tough life lessons. Severe burns, shattered elbows, a broken leg, ACL repair, and dislocated shoulders are just small parts of the challenges that life has thrown at me.

This book is the story of how I harnessed my inner strength, designed my own physical rebound, and discovered mental resilience through pursuing extreme sports. I have learned through experience that when faced with the impossible, there is always a way to make things possible. Our bodies, minds, and spirits have an immense capacity to make us better; we just need to find our way. The first step is to believe the impossible is possible.

From winning the Death Race (one of the hardest outdoor adventure races on the planet), to being crowned World Barefoot Waterski Champion, and onto years as a professional snowboarder, my life pulsed with focus, determination, and mastery, but was not without immense hurdles.

And then I hit rock bottom...

From a place of being paralyzed by years of suppressed trauma—suffering from PTSD—I was able to regain control and rise up...again and again.

This is my story.

My injuries and subsequent recoveries have enabled me to find the strength, experience, and mental fortitude to accomplish things in life that I may otherwise not have. Throughout, I have repeatedly heard that what I was about to do was impossible. Then I went out and did it.

This book is about my journey through life: what I've found, how I've healed, and the ways that I've bounced back repeatedly from the savage beatings life has dealt me. This is how I beat the impossible.

THE HELICOPTER CRASH

IN 1990, I WAS TWENTY YEARS OLD AND IN THE BEST SHAPE of my life, travelling the world as an elite, sponsored snowboarder. Everything I owned fit in the back of my sports car, and I was awash in money and opportunity.

I had just finished competing in a snowboard race at Lake Louise, Alberta, where I had won the mogul competition and the half-pipe. I was sitting on top of the world. Next up was the Snowboard Powder 8 Championships at Mike Wiegele Helicopter Skiing in the northern interior of BC. Living the dream, I packed up my car and drove the five hours to Blue River.

The Powder 8 competition is put on by Mike Wiegele, and the idea is to make a perfectly shaped 8 down the mountain in the powder snow while in perfect unison with your partner. Snowboarding competitors are judged upon speed, shape of turn, size of turn, and how in-sync the pair is.

This was to be the first-ever all-snowboard Powder 8 competition. Until now, the event had been mainly skiers and sometimes one pair of snowboarders. This meant that on that day, some of the top snowboard competitors in the world would be in attendance. I was pretty sure I could win the event.

It was a gorgeous spring day. We were atop the Cariboo Mountains, one of Canada's most amazing glacier zones. The helicopter was loaded up as we geared to go back up for the second run of the event. The chopper was filled with friends—there were thirteen of us.

Soon after takeoff there was a horrible grinding and ripping noise, and the helicopter flipped over in the snow. Immediately someone was yelling "FIRE!" This happened so fast that there was very little time to register that we had just crashed.

Within seconds, the cabin filled with thick, black smoke and flames. It became a race against time to exit the engulfed wreckage. The blaze started to consume us, and the air was a toxic fog.

Memories of the incident come in slow motion. They are truncated, flickering glimpses—snatches of moments broken up in time, sequence, and action...many are missing, having gone up in flames...

I remember not being able to get my seatbelt undone and feeling trapped. That was probably because the buckle was around behind me, as the aircraft was sitting on its side in the snow and I was twisted in my seat. There was a hot flash that ripped through the cabin, and I must have blacked out as most of my memory fades at that point.

I do recall a comfortable, cozy feeling taking over me. It had the feel of being relaxed and wrapped up in a nice warm comforter. All I would have to do is close my eyes and gently drift off to sleep.

It was at that point that I was yanked back to reality, because someone outside the helicopter was yelling "SCHWARTY!" at top volume.

This is when memory kicks back in. I looked around, yelled "Get me the hell out of here!" and blasted out of my seat like a rocket. From the green glow of the skylight, I knew I had gone forward in the machine and was now in the cockpit. How I got there so fast is still a mystery as I never did get my seat-belt undone, and there was only a tiny little space between the headrests and the roof that I rocketed through to get out of the back. The waist of my suit was not burnt, so I must have broken through the seatbelt on my way out as well. Amazing how an adrenaline surge can create superhuman strength.

The next flash of memory is walking through the snow and away from the helicopter as people were staring at me in total horror. I drew my fingers up to my face, discovered how burnt I was, and immediately dropped face-first into the snow. I lay there for a bit as people ran over to help, extinguishing my hair, which was still on fire. My head was a burning ball.

Moments after exiting the helicopter.
This was the first realization of how badly I was burned.
Photo: Ron Dahlquist

Time went in and out of balance over the next few hours, and a lot of it I've pieced together after talking with everyone else who was there. Some of it is my memory, and some are things I think I remember—but they might just be stories from others that have burned into my memory now, so I think of them as my own.

I lay incapacitated in the snow for over an hour before another helicopter arrived to help. I was evacuated first as I was the most seriously hurt of the survivors. There were three friends who did not make it out of the helicopter.

I mostly only recall brief snippets of conversation with people over that time, as I was drifting in and out of consciousness, but I do remember the look on people's faces every time I opened my eyes. It was terror, as though they were looking at someone who was going to die. Well, I sure as hell knew I wasn't going to die, so now I had to reassure everyone else that I was going to make it out alive.

The rescue helicopter flew us back to town, where there were doctors standing by to help. Later, one of the guides told me that on the flight down he'd been sure I was going to die on the flight, but then I opened my eyes and gave him a big thumbs up (which I don't remember at all), and at that point he knew I was going to live.

The air ambulance made a brief stop in Blue River where I was stabilized and had an IV administered.

I was then put back in the helicopter and flown to the next hospital, a hundred kilometres away. Apparently, the helicopter pilot was told to land at the edge of town and they would send an ambulance, but he took one look at me and said that was not going to happen. He radioed in that they needed to clear the parking lot, because he was landing at the front door of the hospital. (In 1990, you could get away with that kind of thing, whereas today you might lose your pilot's license for it.)

The next twenty-four hours were a blur. I fleetingly recall some events, while others, not at all.

They brought me to the hospital in Clearwater, BC. I remember the nurse telling me that they were going to put a catheter into my bladder. I opened one eye and asked where they stuck the needle in to do that, and she politely responded by saying the tube went in my penis. I was twenty years old. That is an outhole. Too late. It was done (and was an experience I wish never to have to repeat).

On the bed beside me was my good friend Karl Achenbach, who had also been in the crash. I heard him hop off the bed and ask if he wouldn't need a catheter if he could pee on his own. He was standing in front of the toilet and mumbling things about waterfalls, rivers, running water...and then I heard him pee and start cheering! This was one of the funniest things I can remember. Maybe it was the drugs they put in me, but I couldn't stop laughing at him. And that's when I vomited.

When the body is burned, the self-preservation instinct shunts all the fluid to the burnt skin area to help cool the burn, so my body robbed all the fluid from my intestinal tract and moved it to my head. That's why when I puked, out came one solid log of undigested food. I laughed even harder. Vomit is supposed to go splat, and not thud onto the floor.

The scene in the room was surreal: two people had just been flown in with serious burns after a devastating helicopter crash. There had been three fatalities, and the casualties were severe and many. And now, here, one of them was hopping around naked trying to go pee, and the other was laughing because he just puked up his lunch.

I knew I was not going to die.

This is the mentality that is needed to face adversity. Everything in life is a choice, and you get to choose how you react to the situation. It's the "oh woe is me" attitude, or "I'll make the best of it!" Your choice. Nobody else can make it for you, but it will certainly have a huge impact on your outcome from the situation. It also has a large influence on those who are treating you. If you believe you will live, then the doctors will believe that as well.

From the time I was a small child, I always knew that I would be able to go through incredible trauma and survive. How I knew this I still do not know. It was a feeling that was always there from the time I can remember. Apparently, I was learning that was true, and that maybe it was the moment I had always known was coming. Not a good time to linger on the thought, but I have certainly examined it further since.

At that moment, I chose to believe I was going to live. What I was sure of was that I was not dead, and I just had to make it out of this alive. Since I hadn't died in the fire, I was certainly not going to die from the trauma hours later.

This was also the time that I learned that three of my friends did not make it out of the helicopter. Neil Daffern, Patty Petrone, and Danny Leblanc were all trapped inside of the burning wreck. Knowing that I was the last survivor to exit the aircraft was a powerful motivator to keep living. Sadly, that was not the time to mourn their loss, as my current survival needs were taking centre stage.

With eyes swelling shut, I overheard the ER staff discussing which burn unit I was going to be sent to. Luckily, I didn't have an intubation tube in my airway yet, and I could still talk. I was coherent enough to tell them that I wanted to be transferred to the Calgary unit, not Vancouver (despite its proximity to Whistler). My parents lived in Calgary, and I knew I was going to be there for an extended length of time (by my standards).

Into the ambulance I went, and off to Kamloops we drove. Then I was loaded into a private plane and flown to Calgary. Can you believe my ambulance bill for a one hundred kilometre trip was more expensive than the private plane to Calgary? This never ceases to amaze me. What's even more amazing is that some thirty years later, I met the pilot who flew me to Calgary that day. What are the chances of that?

My mom and dad were waiting for me at the hospital in Calgary. I was ushered into the ICU for further stabilization and examination to diagnose whether I had any burn injuries to my eyes or lungs. Pointed attention was placed on determining the condition of my eyes as well as trying to discover what had happened to my contact lenses. This, of all the problems, had an easy answer. On the mountainside while waiting for the evacuation helicopter, I had been smart enough to ask a friend to take my contact lenses out for me. That's me—always thinking ahead.

I also remember telling someone (who?) they would need to get my car home, and that the keys were on the dresser in my room in Blue River and the radar detector was under the seat. Should they need to buy gas or dinner on the drive, my wallet was beside the keys. At the time, it had seemed like one of the more important details.

After the medical team had stuffed an intubation tube down my throat to keep me breathing, I had no ability to speak. We played a quick game of charades with them guessing what the heck I was mimicking. Eventually they figured out I wanted a pen and a pad of paper. I recall writing down "Outta here, 1 week." I had no idea how bad I looked, but their response didn't quite match up with my enthusiasm. This was just the start of my foray into miraculous healing, and I didn't have all the tools in my toolbox yet.

I was the lone occupant of the Foothills Hospital Burn Unit, right up to the point when Karl showed up in the room next to me. I couldn't speak yet, as I had breathing tubes down my throat, but Karl could yell at me from next door. His hands had been badly burnt and were wrapped up to his elbows like an Egyptian mummy's.

I couldn't see yet, as my eyes were still swollen shut. They would remain like this for several days, but Karl would audio-describe what was going on. His narrations paid much attention to the wonderful nurse who came in to give me a sponge bath every day.

On the third day, the breathing tube was removed from my lungs, and I was finally able to drink a glass of water. To this day, a glass of cold water is still the most amazing experience in life. It's little things like that I find the most joy in now.

My will to survive was not to be dissuaded by the doctor's prognosis of my life-threatening injuries.

For a full week, I could not open my eyes, so I can only describe what others told me I looked like. Since my body fluid had gone to my head to fight the burn, my head had swelled up to the size of a basketball. I was unrecognizable. One friend said he came to the burn unit to pay me a visit, looked in my room, and saw someone with a balloon-shaped head, crispy and black. He swiftly snuck out, as there was no way that could have been me because that guy looked like he would soon be dead.

Plastic surgeons came in and informed me that my nose and ear were so severely burned that they would fall off. Both the ear and the nose were hard like charcoal. In reassuring tones, the doctors told me not to worry, that they could build me a new nose and ear.

I, however, felt that more surgery and replacing an ear was going to take a horrifically long time. This would keep me in the hospital, at the very least for another month and probably more. That just did not fit into my plans. Not to mention that I had no idea how they could possibly make me an ear and nose out of plastic. That and trying to picture how I would look without a nose or ear were not directions in which I wanted to go. I had to get back to Whistler to finish off my last snowboard competition of the season. I did not have time to stay in the hospital, so nose and ear replacement was not an option. My motivation to heal fast was all-encompassing.

I told the surgeons that I would keep my nose and ear, and that I would be able to heal them and regrow them all on my own. They tried repeatedly to explain why that was not possible. And I tried over and over to explain exactly how I was going to rebuild my own ear and nose. The surgeons sent in counsellors to try to help with my inability to face reality.

Maybe it was the massive doses of morphine I was on, or maybe it was just the attitude of a twenty-year-old professional snowboarder who had just survived a helicopter crash, but either way I was convinced I could rebuild my body parts. One thing I knew for sure—I had nothing to lose by trying. I was going to be stuck in the hospital for at least a month, and I was not good at sitting on my butt and doing nothing. I need to be doing something, otherwise I feel like I'm just wasting the day.

Several years before, I had been reading a surfer magazine, and there was a story about a surfer named Mark Foo. He had broken his femur while surfing in Hawaii and was told he would be in a cast for six to eight weeks. He replied that he needed to be back in a surf contest in six weeks and would take care of his own healing. After two days, he cut off his cast and went to work on rebuilding the bones. He used special visualization techniques where he pictured the bones growing back together one cell at a time. He did this almost all day long. As his other main healing methods, he added acupuncture and nutrition. And, six weeks later, he was back surfing the massive North Shore waves, healed up and charging full speed. This was going to be me.

Now it was time to walk the talk, build myself a new ear and nose, and show the doctors that I could do what was deemed to be impossible.

I spent every spare moment in my hospital room doing the exact same visualization that Foo had described. I was on morphine, and it's amazing what you can believe is real when you're already having an out-of-body experience.

I personalized the technique, picturing little green men going from the core of my body, carrying little balls of green energy, and rebuilding the skin one cell at a time. I envisioned them taking away the burnt skin. Hours upon hours were used as the green men would reconnect the nerves, attach the skin, build more cartilage, and generally do everything that was possible to build me my body new parts. I believed in this so strongly that there was only one possible outcome from it, and that was success.

Doctors came in each day and kept telling me they were just waiting for the ear and nose to fall off so they could construct the new ones. I kept telling them that my nose and ear were not going to fall off, and that I was working on it all on my own. They kept telling me it was impossible, and I kept telling them it was not. I started to enjoy their visits, as it renewed my focus and belief in what I was doing. Sometimes motivation shows up in the strangest of ways. Being told I can't do something seems to be the best driving tool to get me to do something.

After two weeks, I was off the morphine, and I found I was able to maintain longer and more powerful visualization sessions. I had a specific goal in mind, and I had the burning (pun intended) desire to achieve that goal. I would not fail.

By week three, the doctors came in and acknowledged that my nose and ear were somehow regrowing. They told me this should not be possible, and they still might fall off. But still, I seemed to be overcoming the impossible.

Largely I was being motivated by the Ocean Pacific Pro Snowboard Series competition, forthcoming in Whistler. I needed to get to that race in two months and defend my title. There was no way I was giving Alex Warburton and Jason Ford a free ride to the podium. I was going to recover, rebuild, prepare, and get back on the snow to compete. I hadn't worked as hard as I had all winter just to be stuck in the hospital. I was still going to live—and perpetually chase—the dream.

While living in the burn unit, I went through several skin grafts and surgeries to replace the severely burnt skin areas on my face, neck, and wrist. Some elements of the day's process were painless—others excruciating. One round of skin grafts sticks out above all.

On day ten in the hospital, I was being prepped for a major set of skin grafts. My left leg and thigh had been shaved and ready as the donor site, while the rest of my face, neck, and wrist had been roughed up and was awaiting the skin transplant. The idea was to peel off the skin from the leg with what looked to be a giant cheese peeler. Later that day, the skin would be rolled back down on my face and neck in hopes that the body would accept the new skin and not have to go through the scarring process. During the day, the transplant sites were covered in gauze with sterile water to keep them moist.

That evening, the gauze was gently peeled back, and the new skin was placed on the slightly weeping burns. The grafts were gently rolled down, and then it was just time to wait for the body to accept the new skin as though it had always been there. The only thing the doctors forgot was to moisten the gauze that had been on my wrist during the day. With such a focus on my face and neck, somehow the wrist got overlooked. Just before the surgeons were leaving my room, they realized that the wrist needed to be done. I even remember the discussion amongst them that the gauze was dry and hard, and this was not good.

That was when they yanked the dried gauze off the fresh third-degree burn on my wrist.

During the day, the gauze had managed to imbed itself into the wound and attach itself to all the nerves that were exposed from the prepping work on the burn. Once the gauze had been unceremoniously yanked off, it took all the skin with it, as well as exposing every one of the nerves underneath. The pain hit like a sledgehammer. How much pain? Imagine having the nerves in your teeth being drilled on without any freezing and then the drill bit hits the nerve. Then multiply that pain level by a thousand.

My mouth was open to scream, yet no sound came out other than muted grunts. The pain level was so intense that at first I was sure I would just pass out—I would wake up later and it would be all good. That did not happen for me. Instead, the pain escalated, and I grabbed onto the steel bed rail with my other hand and squeezed it as though I was transferring all my pain into the bed frame. That pain level remained for at least two minutes while the surgeons put the new graft onto my wrist. As soon as they finished, wrapped my wrist up, and the pain subsided, I collapsed back on the bed in a full sweat and immediately fell asleep.

The next morning, I looked at the rail on the bed where I had been holding onto it and realized how intense the pain had been. I had bent the entire bedrail into a pretzel. I mumbled silent prayers to never go through pain like that again in my life.

Friends visited almost every day. They drove out from Whistler, and they flew in from the US. Get-well cards arrived from every corner of the earth. I'd really had no idea I had so many good friends around the world who cared so deeply for me. This support from friends and family was a monster-sized step in my motivation to heal up and get back into my life as fast as possible. The outpouring of love and concern brought a tear to my eye every day. I still have most of their letters.

Healing can be severely stunted by the mind, if one's attitude is negative and dark. The body reacts quite strongly to one's underlying belief. Attitude is—and becomes—everything.

Occupational therapists came to visit, to talk about what I would need for the next few years of burn rehabilitation. This was not a short-term injury, and it would need constant attention for the rest of my life to keep the scars under control, keeping them from shrinking and disfiguring my face.

In the process of scar management and healing, I was most surprised by how the Jobst garments were used. These are super-tight nylon stockings custom made to go over the body. I was given one for my arm, and one that would cover my whole head and face. The latter had a big Velcro closure going up the back of the head. Yes, that face you are making right now was the exact same reaction I had. This was serious news; I would need to wear this bank robber's mask, and I was in for a lifetime of rehab. If ever there was a moment to feel sorry for myself, this would have been it. I had figured I would be out of the hospital, on my way home, and life would move on like nothing had happened. But it wasn't going to go that way.

Looking in the mirror, it was easy to see how badly I'd been deformed and how long and hard the way forward was going to be. I have never been someone who falls into the oh-woe-is me attitude, but I could see how easily it could happen. Thoughts began to circulate. I wondered if I would ever find anyone who would want to date me. She would have to either be a solid human being or a total freak. This certainly brought fresh emotions, and I did shed some tears. It could have easily been a tipping point into despair for me. Luckily, I decided that the pity-party was not part of who I am, or ever was. Every day from here forward was going to be the best day of my life. I had seen the worst day, and in every additional day of life, I would be living—and continuing to live—the dream. I do this to this day.

The physiotherapy team told me that I would need the mask on for at least a year and maybe more, depending on how the scars healed up. The idea of the mask was to act like a top layer of skin to keep pressure on all the scar tissue and help it grow flat and smooth. Otherwise scar tissue grows in a keloid manner, which is to say like a giant knot as it becomes hard and non-flexible and pulls the skin around in all sorts of grotesque manners. This also meant that I would have to do constant stretching, pulling, massaging, and just general mashing of the scar tissue as it formed, in order to break it down and allow it to be soft and supple. Hard work up front for a few years, and then less work for the rest of my life.

Wearing this head stocking for a year was not something I was looking forward to. I knew I'd have to send someone into the banks or stores ahead of me wherever I went, so as not to freak people out when a masked bandit was entering their business. On the other hand, I would have the best Halloween costume ever. Finding the good from this was difficult at the time, but after many long discussions with the physio crew, they decided we could experiment with a full-face, clear-plastic mask instead of the nylon stocking. Now, this sounded cool! At least it sounded like an improvement over the other option. I was voluntarily testing the apparatus and would be the first person in the world to wear it. The hope was that it would keep the skin from drying out as much while it kept pressure on the scar tissue. I'd still wear the head stocking at night and when going swimming (which was thankfully still permitted). I'd already come to grips with the fact that "looking normal" was not something that would be in my life for a very long time, if ever.

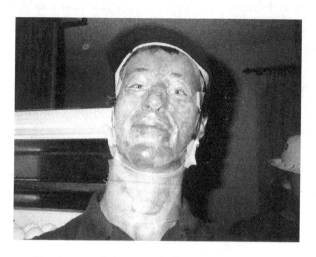

The plastic mask that I wore for four years. Photo: Mom

The burn-unit nurses were angels. They did an amazing and exacting job of keeping the infection out and constantly peeling the dead and burnt skin away. They took exceptional care of me. I'll never be able to give enough credit to the phenomenal humans that treat with such care the hideous-pain-wracked wrecks of humans that they work on in there. I am eternally grateful.

Karl and I treated the burn ward like our private party center. From answering the nurses' phone, "Hello, burn unit. Chief burn victim speaking. How may I help you?" to ordering-in pizza. One day, when I had several friends visiting, I rang the buzzer to call the nurse. When she arrived, I waved my arms around like the King of England and asked for a round of apple juice for all my friends. She walked away laughing. Yet no apple juice arrived. The poor nurses put up with a lot but had great senses of humour to tolerate the number of visitors we had.

I was 190 pounds when I entered the hospital and had shriveled to 150 when I got out. It's amazing how many calories your body will consume when you're trying to rebuild all your skin. How anyone can survive in a hospital by eating hospital food is beyond my comprehension. I have never seen food cooked so poorly or taste worse than a TV dinner. After a week, I gave up ordering from their list of hideously overcooked slop and rawhide consistency meats and just asked friends to bring in food. Ken Achenbach came in daily with a double burger from Pete's Drive-in and a root beer shake. I looked forward to that gourmet meal more than anything else. Later, my mom and dad would arrive with roast beef and Cheezies. I was discovering that food was a major element in keeping my positive attitude up, and my friends and family were essential in making this happen.

I lived in the hospital for four weeks until all my open wounds had healed to the point that they were no longer at risk of infection. Then I was given the green light to go home.

Packing up my room took most of the day. The nurses relayed that they had seen people in there for eight months who had not collected as much stuff as I had. There was a video game console, a giant stereo system, a stack of weights, boxes of cards, bundles of flowers, plus tons of books and magazines. It looked like I had moved in for good. I really believe that it was all these little things that kept me in a positive frame of mind. I was surrounded emotionally and materially with support.

I stayed with my parents for another month. Daily visits to the physiotherapy clinic were required, as well as multiple minor skin grafts and hair transplants. Both of my eyebrows had been burnt off, and it looked like they were not going to regrow themselves. I had never thought of using the little green men to plant new eyebrows! Damn.

During that time, I trained as hard as I possibly could to get myself back in proper snowboarding physical shape. That month in the hospital had severely taken me down from the prime physical stature that I had been in. Forty pounds lost in a month do not come back overnight, and even now I'm pretty sure I've still not recovered the same-size quads I had previously.

On my return to Whistler, I was given a monstrous reception by all my friends. They threw me a party that lasted for days. This support was a realization that I was on the right track and surrounded by the right people.

Snowboarding started up again as soon as Whistler opened for the summer season. I had one month before the finals of the Ocean Pacific Pro, and I was going to be ready.

It wasn't until I got myself back on the snow that I finally realized what a tough road I had ahead. I was physically weak, my strength was down by fifty percent, and I may not have admitted it at the time, but I was certainly a long way from where my peak performance needed to be. While sitting on the top of the mountain, I had to have a few conversations with myself to remind myself that I had all the skills and all the potential and that nobody else was going to do it for me but me. If I was going to be back on the top of the world with my snowboarding, then I had better take my own advice and start truly believing it myself.

Race day came, and although I was still only 160 pounds, I felt I had done everything possible to be ready for the race.

There were three different events for the weekend. The half-pipe was first, then the moguls, followed up by the giant slalom. Moguls were the one event where I truly felt nobody in the world would ever beat me, and this weekend was my chance to prove it again.

When I had learned to snowboard at Sunshine Village, in Banff, Alberta, I was usually the only snowboarder on the hill, and most skiers did not want to hang out with a snowboarder. The only people who would ride with me were the Alberta Freestyle Ski Team. Being outcasts of the ski industry themselves, they thought I fit right in. They liked skiing moguls, and they did not care if they ditched me. This meant that if I wanted someone to ride with, I would have to learn to snowboard through moguls and do it fast. I realize that this method of learning to snowboard helped every aspect of my career, as everything in snowboarding is easy after riding moguls.

In the half-pipe event, I managed a top-ten finish and was happy despite not taking home a medal. Due to an intense storm with wind and lightning, the mogul event had to be cancelled. While the moguls were the event that I had really been looking forward to, I knew I would have to play my A-game to vie for the title. This left only the giant slalom to determine the winner of the OP Pro Tour. Jason and Alex were certainly not going down without a fight. With the difference in points, it looked like it might not be possible to knock Jason out of first place, but I would certainly make the day hard on Alex.

Race day was warm, wet, and slushy on the top of the mountain and we were all excited to get the battle underway. I may talk about how excited I was to be competing and how much I wanted to win, but in the end, I was just having another fun day of snowboarding with my good friends. At the end of the first run, I behind Jason and Alex, and I needed to make up at least two seconds on the second run.

Try as I might, I remained out of the top five in the giant slalom and was unable to scrape back those two seconds that I needed. This meant that the overall OP Pro title went to Jason, with Alex in second, and me standing in third.

I was so happy it's almost impossible to explain.

From where I had been in the hospital only three months prior, to being back on the snow and pulling off a third overall, was nothing short of miraculous in my mind. If I could do this, then in my mind I could do anything.

THE DEATH RACE

THERE ARE VERY FEW TIMES IN A PERSON'S LIFE WHERE ONE gets to find out what one is made of without being in a real life-or-death situation. It is also rare to intentionally put yourself into a situation where it seems that death would be better than what you are doing. For me, this experience was the Death Race.

How did I get into something as ludicrous as a race where the website for the event was titled youmaydie.com? Easy. In 2010, a friend who is on the FBI Hostage Rescue Team called me up, telling me all about an incredible competition that would push me to my limits and beyond. He said, "It will crush you like a bug and make you want to beg for Momma." This was his description of a race where the whole intent is to break you physically and mentally until you quit. It's a test, where the rules change depending on who you are and how much the organizers want to see you suffer. You will never know exactly how long it will be, what you will be doing, where you will be going, or how long it will be between your next bites of food. It's a race that in the previous year had only a two-percent finish rate out of 300 racers.

I asked my friend Benjamin why he had phoned me specifically.

"I made a list of all the people I know who would go in this race with me...and finish it."

"Did you call them?"

"I did." And after a long pause, he said, "You are the only name on the list."

Five minutes later, I was signing up for one of the most daunting races on the planet.

An outdoor-adventure race normally begins with competitors reviewing the course ahead of time. You get to prepare for its intricacies, learn what you will be doing, and be able to gauge how long the race is going to take you. The Death Race, on the other hand, is not like that at all. You really have zero information about the race in advance, other than it'll be hard, and you'll want to quit. Nothing more...except for its general location—in this case, Pittsfield, Vermont. But the race's exact starting point or time remained a mystery.

Over a period of two months, the gear list was slowly given out. Some bits of information appeared on Facebook, some came directly from the organizers, and other info was emailed out. The "official" start time was not fully announced until about the week before, and even then, it was flexible. That is the mind game that the organizers (Joe Desana and Andy Wineberg) like to play.

Priority one was to check out all the videos and information I could source. In 2010, online sites and information networks were less robust than we find today. Everything I uncovered showed a grueling, twenty-four-hour event that combined both mental and physical challenges in the worst possible manner and combinations. I took careful note that there was always a part about chopping firewood. The person who took a little hatchet never finished the race. I would need a good axe. Luckily, I love chopping wood.

The organizers and course crew were not there to motivate you in any way, shape, or form. The videos showed them telling people about how miserable they must be, how the blisters would rot through their feet, and why they should just quit and go home. Words of encouragement were non-existent. My own cohort of athletic friends—and the stunts we did together—had prepared me for this race better than any training I could have done.

PREPARE, PREPARE, PREPARE...AND PREPARE AGAIN

In order to succeed, I knew I needed a support crew. Though I would have Benjamin by my "competitive side," I needed to find someone to help me out with food, logistics, beer, photography, cheerleading, and to be there simply to watch the miserable event. Benjamin would arrange the same. I talked my friend Christian Hrab into this nasty job, and he came along willingly. Christian lived in Montreal, Québec me, in Whistler, British Columbia. I would fly out east to join him; then all we needed to do was head south, cross the border, and drive to Vermont.

Christian knew me well. He had been my boardercross coach for several years, and he understood what makes me tick and how to motivate me when needed. Not only do the Death Race organizers play mind games with the racers, but they also mess with the support crews. Support people aren't given any valuable clues. Neither are they provided with any details on how the racers are doing in the field. Most of the time they really have no idea where the racers are until they hit a checkpoint in the mountains. (We were not equipped with GPS trackers while competing.)

Sometimes, the support crews were sent off on mad journeys through the mountains—Christian can attest—as a way to mess with them. Why would they leave all that fun traipsing through the mountainside to just the racers?

As far as the internet could tell me, the race started in the town of Pittsfield, then we'd head into the hills for unknown amounts of time, consistently returning to the possible starting point, a local farm. (As I found out, it did not always go quite this way.) At that point, racers should be able to restock food, put on dry clothes, mend blisters, tell stories, or just quit and go home. The race always involved brutal hikes through the mountains while carrying heavy objects, a lot of time being wet and miserable at night in the mountains while carrying excessively heavy objects, and the not-to-be-forgotten copious amounts of firewood chopping.

One of the main goals of the event was to find out what you were capable of mentally, after being systematically broken down physically. Many of the tasks during the race were to challenge one's mental capabilities and memory after grueling bouts of intense physical exercise.

I set up my training to prepare for most of the unknowns. I had read enough Navy Seals books to understand that the more you bleed in practice, the less you bleed in action. The first purchase was a fifty-pound weight vest. I figured I'd better learn how to run, walk, climb, and just plain live in the vest for the months leading up to the race. I would put the equivalent of a ten-year-old child on my back in the morning and would not take it off until the end of the day. (As a result, I vowed that I would do everything in my power to never become fifty pounds overweight.) Wearing that thing all day, every day, was a special kind of misery. The only saving grace was that I got to take it off every night.

My custom training regime looked a lot like a CrossFit workout on steroids. I started by doing an 800-metre sprint around my block and returned to the house after each lap to do fifty reps of a different exercise. I thought I should put in as many varied and nasty exercises that I could think of, just to be sure.

Lap 1: 50 pull ups.

Lap 2: 50 heavy weight squats.

Lap 3: 50 sit ups with a 20-pound medicine ball.

Lap 4: 50 walking lunges.

Lap 5: 50 burpees.

Lap 6: 50 burpees (no, not a typo...I just enjoy the punishment)

Lap 7: 50 box jumps.

Lap 8: 50 push-ups.

Lap 9: 50 ball slams.

I would continue this for at least twenty laps, and all this would usually take me two hours.

Rain or shine, five days a week, this regime was followed. After a few weeks the neighbours began sitting on their deck, drinking beer and cheering me on while I ran laps around the house in the pouring two-degree Celsius rain.

Three days a week I put on the vest and ran to the base of the ski hill, where I would find a nice twenty-pound rock. With rock in hand, I jogged up to the top of the first chairlift, about 1200 vertical feet, and dumped my rock in an ever-growing pile. To increase the intensity of the workout, I decided while going uphill on the ski run I would do ten push-ups every time I found money on the ground. This was a very bad idea. The first day I found eight dollars in change, and I did about 300 push-ups. After that, I chose only to do push-ups when I found a dollar or more.

The hill-running regime started at six a.m., and often it was cold and wet. Running alone in the rain when it is cold is an intense internal battle. It would be easy to only go halfway up, or take a smaller rock, or no rock at all. Who would know? I would know, and that was not acceptable. Part of this event was showing my kids that we can do anything we set our minds to, but we have to be willing to make the sacrifice to succeed. Some of these sacrifices had to be paid with sweat and suffering.

The gear list for the Death Race was random at best: knitting needles, a five-gallon pail, a hand drill, a hat, safety goggles, pen and paper, and about twenty other (often) useless items. Most of the gear was never used. That said, I *did* spend a lot of time learning how to knit before going. By the time I loaded my pack, put in dry clothes, repair kits, Band-Aids, Krazy Glue, food, water, and everything else I thought I might need, the bag tipped the scales at just over fifty pounds. That was the same as the weight vest I'd worn for the past few months.

There was a labyrinth of emails, Facebook posts, and other endless speculations to comb through to determine when and where the Death Race would start. I finally concluded that we would meet at the church in Pittsfield at four p.m. With our travel schedule, this meant I had the day to explore the small town, talk to the other racers, get the lay of the land, and make sure that my maps had all the local landmarks. Rumours were spreading like wildfire. Excitement was in the air. Every story you could possibly imagine was out there, from the race being cancelled, to an entirely new gear list having just been released, to the organizers holding court in front of the general store disclosing "secrets" and hints. In response, I did the opposite of fretting about things, went for a drive out of town, and enjoyed an awesome lunch of Irish stew, butter, and beer. Packing in as many calories as I possibly could before the race seemed like a wise idea. I was calm, thinking I was prepared, and above, the sky threatened to rain.

The congregation of competitors, and their respective cheering squads, gathered at church at four o'clock. Each year the race has a different theme. This year it was religion. And oh, *the theatrics*! I loved it! From loving prayers by the "pastor" to outright yelling and screaming, the organizers-cum-preachers fired up the fear wagon like I've never seen. I actually began questioning my level of preparedness. If they could do this to *me*, then I was wondering how many of the others were questioning their own levels of readiness. Together, at this moment, I think we may have been questioning our sanity...more than just a little.

I had not given any thought to the concept of winning. I just wanted to go and see what I was truly capable of. I had a pretty good idea of what I could do, but this would be one of the first true tests of my abilities. Truth was, in this race, the focus was not so much on winning as it was about finishing. Completion was the main goal.

Yes, I'd run ten-kilometre races before, done the CrossFit Games, and was in the best shape of my life, but this was the first time I would really test what I could do for twenty-four hours or longer. At least, the year before it had been twenty-four hours, but I just assumed they would make it harder than that.

I checked out the competition. There were people of all sizes and shapes, Navy Seals, and marathoners. There were women and men. More men, though, than women. Some looked like world-champion athletes, and some looked like last week was the first time in their lives they had ever exercised. The field was diverse, to say the least. I looked at the Navy Seal, who was 250 pounds of pure muscle, and thought I might not be well prepared enough. I caught myself judging someone I deemed one hundred pounds overweight, wondering why they were there. I did the visual assessment of most everyone. In doing so, I was assessing those I thought might be able to finish this race, and I was pretty sure everyone was doing the same thing. In the end, I found that none of this evaluation made one lick of difference, as the physical component was only twenty percent of what this race was about. This race was—and is—about who you are mentally, and not who you are physically, as I soon found out.

Three hundred people were at the church for the racers' meeting. We had to walk two miles down the side of the highway to get to the farm where the race would start. At that time, at least ten people dropped out of the race and went home. It seemed that they'd had no idea what kind of race they'd signed up for and were probably making the wise decision.

Sadly, in a last-minute twist, Benjamin had been unable to join me in the race. He was owner of Ski Santa Fe in New Mexico, and one week before, there'd been a monstrous forest fire burning near his ski hill. Now, he was on fire-suppression duty all day and night, because there was a significant possibility that the fire would overrun his resort.

The night before I was to get on the plane to go to the Death Race, I phoned Benjamin to see if I was heading the wrong direction—if I should instead be going to New Mexico to help him. Benjamin said he had it mostly under control, and the addition of one more person would not change the outcome of the fire. He told me to go to the Death Race, and to make sure I finished.

Suddenly not having Benjamin at my side for this event was a major mental let-down. I had really been looking forward to having a good friend by my side while I suffered in the mountains. Now, I was second guessing being in the race.

I remember my thought process very clearly at this point, and it was not a feeling of triumph and success. In fact, it felt more like a foreboding doom and gloom. The skies were grey, it was about to rain, I had a total of zero friends with me as we were separated from our support crew, and I was questioning every decision I had made about being in the race.

Getting beyond this point of self-destructive thought was going to take a monumental effort. I needed to get out of this head space in order to finish.

I tried to sort out what the best line of attack would be going solo in the race, instead of hanging out with Benjamin. The more I thought about it, the worse my attitude got. I would need to do a 180-degree turn mentally and take this as an opportunity to show myself that I could still do anything.

And that's what I did. Letting Benjamin down at this point would be horrible, and I knew he would never let me live it down. In order to celebrate his decision to stay home, I would go and finish this race and bring back epic tales of struggle and sacrifice. I was finding the driving force from the need to show Benjamin that his belief in me was not misplaced.

It really doesn't matter where you find your motivation, as long as you have it. Without motivation, there is little to keep your personal drive going, and when things get challenging, it becomes all too easy to give up. What I really needed was to make some new friends and enjoy the race I was in.

Part of my preparation for the event had been watching and studying motivational movies, video clips, and books to glean every ounce of personal drive and fortitude that I could. One scene in a film stood out in which a coach talked only about giving your best—whatever your best was. Give only your best, but nothing less than your best. I stuck that thought in my head and trudged forward, now knowing I would do exactly that. I would not stop until I knew I had done my best. At least then I could face Benjamin and tell him I had put in my full 100%.

To call this event a "race" is not really being honest. It was part race, part beatdown, and part mental torture. It was an exercise in finding out who you were as a person. One competitor said that he got more out of this event than a year of counselling for anger management.

The first portion of the race had nothing to do with racing at all. It was designed to frustrate you, exhaust you, torture you, and show you that you were not prepared. The goal of the organizers was to get you to quit. Quitting would reveal exactly who you were at that moment. It was an opportunity to scrutinize what had driven you to quit, and how to make yourself a tougher person down the road. This race was all about going forward, no matter what the challenge. It was about finding out what breaks you, and breaking you was what they were good at. It was a race of understanding.

I convinced myself I was qualified. I had survived a helicopter crash and four years of burn rehabilitation. My body had been broken, with some disfiguring injuries. The Death Race would be a piece of cake compared to the life I had already lived. I believed that no matter what the race could throw at me, that I had already been through worse, and I was still standing. I also knew that there was a limit to the amount of time that the race could keep volunteers out on the course before they needed to go back to work or fell from exhaustion on their own. It would eventually have an end, and maybe I just needed to outlast the course workers.

At seven p.m., the race started, and it was raining. Not just a little bit of drizzle and mist, but a solid, raging downpour that any rainforest would have been proud of. Everyone had on their fifty-pound packs, and we were soaked.

We had been placed in groups of thirteen to lift rocks in a giant group activity. We were to bend down, pick up a seventy-pound rock, lift it up to our chests, put it back down, and move on to the next rock...and to do it 1653 times. Pick up the mud-covered rock, put it back down, and move over to the next rock. If the person beside you could not lift their rock, we all were tasked to help them do it and then continue. If you dropped the rock, you had to do twenty burpees. The small-framed, eighty-pound woman needed help with every single one of her rock lifts. That alone was just about enough to make a person quit. I made a mental note: in future, try to avoid being in a group with someone, male or female, who can't lift an eighty-pound rock.

I learned quickly not to ask any questions where there might be an easy answer and a hard answer. Then, at least, I'd avoid a reply wherein the answer would lead to an anguishing physical outcome. It was better just to do and not ask. We all found this out the hard way. While doing the wet rock lifts, I took off my fifty-pound pack and set it on the ground. Someone then asked the event marshals if we could do this with our packs off. The answer: "No! Put all your packs back on!" You can imagine how popular that guy was. We were also all given a one hundred burpee penalty. Ever tried to do a hundred burpees in a row? Ever tried to do them in the mud and pouring rain...with that ten-year-old-kid on your back? Trust me, this was about as miserable as the day could get.

During the rock lifting, I went through a myriad of emotional states. From feeling energized and excited, to shivering and miserable, to lonely and tired, to numb and zombie-like, I was encountering them all and not in a good way. I would need people to suffer with if I was going to get through this. As we all know, misery loves company. Luckily there were 300 other people that were probably feeling the exact same thing I was. Thinking about how we had 300 of the world's most unlikely people lifting rocks in the rain made me start to giggle. I realized that I fit in perfectly, and I had 300 friends with me. Then I started to sing children's songs. Having two young daughters at home, I knew them all, and I sang them all. It was surprising how many others joined in with my signing in the rain, and equally as shocking at how many people looked at me like I needed to be removed from the gene pool.

At two a.m., after seven hours of lifting rocks, we were allowed to abandon the rocks. We were told to get in line, walk to the river, and follow it two miles upstream to the next checkpoint. The river walk was to be done in the water. It was pitch dark. If you were to set foot on the bank, you would be disqualified.

Being the eager beaver that I am, I jumped right in, pack on, axe in hand, and wearing my specialized river shoes. (Clearly, I had done a ton of preparatory—and anticipatory – research.)

Hindsight would say I should have checked to see how deep the water was first. I immediately plummeted down, gasping for air through eight feet of water, ending up anchored to the bottom with my well-strapped-on pack. Being in Olympic-caliber shape certainly has its benefits, as I calmly waded upstream about ten metres to a small sandbar I'd spied before going under, where I managed to get my head back above water. It's always amazing to me to have the chance to witness what systems of logic run through one's head when you are about to die. My plunge certainly made the rest of the 270 people enter the water a whole lot slower than I did.

After the first mile, I was in the lead group with about three other guys...one of them being Joe Decker, who held the title of the World's Fittest Man. They had all been in the race before, and were quite eager to talk with me, especially after having just witnessed me jump into the deep end of the river and walk out like it was an everyday event. They all commented that what I had done was so insanely stupid that this must be the perfect event for me.

Mile one found us waiting for the rest of the crew. They were stretched down the river like landing lights on the runway waiting for a 747 to land. I remember feeling annoyed at all the slow movers and having to sit on the side of the riverbank, soaking wet and cold, while we waited for people who had obviously not properly prepared for the race. I remember asking the race veterans how they dealt with it. They said that it was just a stage to suffer through, then when the race started, you would never see them again as they would all be behind you.

In keeping with the religious theme, the river walk was to represent Moses parting the seas, and the next stage had something to do with the Apostles. After a second mile of river sloshing, swimming, and wading, we arrived at the coldest spring-fed pond on the planet. This water had to be only five degrees Celsius in the middle of June.

I know little about religion, but I made a quick assumption that the Apostles were immune to hypothermia, incoherency, and fatigue, but loved to try to keep candles lit in a pouring rain. I made a mental note to find out more about them when the race was over.

For seven laps we had to do a crossing of the freezing pond, then scale a forty-five-degree mud slope, whilst taking a lit candle on a one-mile walk around the farm in the pouring rain. We then had to do it another six times. By the end of the second lap, I was shaking uncontrollably due to hypothermia. I could barely keep the candle lit due to the shaking and was coming close to understanding why it was called the Death Race. If the candle was to go out, we would have to restart the lap around the field. I feared anything that would cause this stage to take even one second longer than it needed to. It would be better to burn holes through my hands keeping the candle lit than to see the last glimmer of heat flicker out.

The pond we crossed was so cold that upon entering and having the water fill every inch of my jacket, I started to involuntarily hyperventilate. This panic breathing did not subside until I exited the other side of the pond. Just knowing that I was coming back to this pond six more times was horrific. Clear thinking goes out the window once the body starts shivering, and that's exactly what I was doing. Wearing shorts, a t-shirt, and a light-weight, waterproof jacket probably did not help, but anything else would be soaked anyway, and then it would just be heavy. There was no correct way to dress for this race.

Christian, my one-person support crew, later said he thought I looked like I might just die after the third lap. I was pale, shaking, incoherent, and my speech was slurred. Christian offered me a thermos of hot coffee and I downed it in one gulp. The caffeine provided the jolt and made me a bit less miserable. That was the turning point of the race for me. My mental attitude picked up, and then it was time to just get back out there and get the job done.

I had experienced life in a state that was far worse than just being cold and miserable. I knew I had to lift myself up from this point, or finishing the race was not going to happen. Making a comeback from rock bottom was what I was good at, and now was the time for me to do it again.

That was Apostle Hell. I had finished the seven laps and didn't die but then found myself sitting on my ass, waiting for those slower, and colder, to finish. Suddenly a group of still mostly strangers found themselves all hugging each other in the mud to try to keep warm. The guy next to me admitted, chuckling, "I just pissed my pants to keep warm." This made me laugh, as I had done the same thing five minutes earlier. Nothing like hugging strangers while pissing yourself and getting a laugh out of it. This is the kind of thing that enables one to get through the Death Race. You either laugh at the miseries or sit down and cry yourself out of the race. And since I knew nobody would care if I cried, I just laughed.

So, apparently, the race component had still not actually started yet. This was still part of the group beat-down, and I was really amazed at how few people had dropped out so far.

For me, I found myself resenting all the people who were slower than me and making me wait for them to catch up. Admittedly, this approach may not have been the best one to reinforce group strength and dynamics. I would need something to spike my attitude and quick.

It was five a.m., and the sun was rising when we began transitioning into the next task. My outlook was perking up with the sunrise. Those first rays of sunshine on the face encouraged me, made me feel that this was entirely possible, that I really would, *or could*, finish this race. Yes, I was grasping at straws, and that was exactly what I needed.

One of the rocks I had to carry for eight hours. Photo: Kasi Armstong Lubin

A Bible verse came next. The task was to pick up a fifty-pound stump and follow the pink ribbons up the side of the mountain. At the top there would be a passage from the Bible. We were to memorize it, follow the orange ribbons back down, and then recite the verse. Get even one word wrong, and we would have to heft the stump back up the steep grades and do a better job of memorizing. Off I went with my fifty pounds of gear and my fifty-pound stump to follow the ribbons up the hill for 1000 vertical feet. I wrote the verse down in my notebook and recited it 500 times while walking back down the trail.

When I got to the next checkpoint, I recited my verse properly and got to sit in the sunshine and wait for everyone else. Some poor sap had to take off back up the hill after saying "man" instead of "men" as the last word of the verse. I was happy not to be that guy...*or man*.

Finally, the race was about to start. We were fourteen hours into it and still waiting for the rest of the slower movers to catch up. At this point, five of us turned to one of the organizers and tried to convince him that we needed to get going—that it wasn't our fault the slow people were so slow. We must have sounded convincing, as he sent us off to the farm by way of the river.

Back at the farm, after much-needed food, clean socks, and dry clothes, we were told to go chop a four-foot log from a massive and horrendous pile of waterlogged poplar. We were to use our hand drill to mark our bib number in the log. My log weighed in at fifty pounds. (That ten-year-old kid kept appearing all through the race! A seemingly reoccurring number.) But this now meant, with the log lashed onto my pack, as was instructed—I was carrying one hundred pounds. If I ever found myself training to do this again, a heavier weight vest would be required,

The adventure races always try to outdo each other with the size of their logs.
Photo: Tough Mudder

Log in tow, the next task was to follow a new line of pink ribbons straight into the uncut forest, up the mountain, down the mountain, across the mountain, and sideways around the mountain...to then turn back down the mountain, bushwhacking with one hundred pounds on my back. I was thoroughly impressed with the nasty bushwhacking the organizers had done to lay out this devious trail.

Halfway through this, my legs hit the wall. I wanted to go farther, but my legs said they had had enough, and it was quitting time. Both quads had seized solid, and I couldn't have walked even if I'd wanted to. This is where I encountered a problem. (There had been many, but this one presented a dilemma.) If I took off my pack, I'd never get it back on. If I put it down, I wouldn't be able to pick it up...it weighed one hundred pounds, for heaven's sake. I was beginning to understand a bit more about religion.

I found a tree that I could lean up against to rest. I got the next person walking by to get my water bottle out, and I drank two litres of water. The next person retrieved my food. I had another feast of my homemade mash of hemp hearts, coconut oil, bacon, nuts, seeds, salt, and cocoa powder. One thousand calories per cup. Just what I needed.

My legs still wouldn't work, but at least I was happy. (Maybe slightly delirious). I waited and waited some more, but still nothing. Then, from the motivational videos I'd watched, I remembered a story about a long-distance runner. He had talked about hitting the wall and how to overcome it. He'd described it as running down the side of the wall until you find an open door, then going through the proverbial wall and continuing. So, I started shuffling up the trail looking for that freaking hole in the wall. Calling it suffering would be an understatement at this point. I knew I had to try to move, but every inch forward was an entirely new level of muscle pain and body ache. The brain was willing, but the body was on strike. I really believe that if I had hit that state near the end of the race, I would not have recovered.

After about twenty minutes of this horrific zombie shuffling, my right leg started to bend, and I could now limp. This was ecstasy. Twenty more minutes, and my left leg started to work. Hot damn! I was back in the race. I'd found the hole in the wall and was moving again. This was not the last time I would find myself needing to use that trick.

YOU BECOME WHAT YOU BELIEVE

The brain is shockingly powerful, and it is rarely more apparent than in an event like the Death Race. My physical self was done. I was out of gas. From then on, I drove forward with mental fortitude and dug into my motivations. Why did I have to continue? If I did not, I'd be letting Benjamin down. What if he had just lost his ski resort to fire, and I told him I gave up because I was tired? This possibility was simply not acceptable to me.

I finished the forest-log-toting section and ended up back at the farm, where we were to throw our logs into the swampy pond. Everyone else's were floating on top. When I threw my log in, it sank like a submarine with screen doors. It disappeared into the murk. At that moment, I wasn't quite sure if I should laugh or cry.

So, I inhaled more food: a one-pound hamburger patty with a quarter pound of butter on top and thick almond butter to hold the whole thing together. This was the nutrient of the Gods... thematically fitting and just as fulfilling.

The Death Race required calories. Lots of them. There was no place for carbohydrates. Once you start on the sugar, you've got to keep it going non-stop for the next twenty-four hours or you'll bonk right out of the race. I was burning 10,000 calories every twelve hours, and your body can only take in about 8000 calories in that time. This means unless you have a significant body fat supply to feed off, you are doomed. Those super-lean marathoners had no chance, as they just did not have enough body fat to burn. Same with the ultra-lean Navy Seal guy. Too heavy, not enough body fat, and no way to eat enough food to keep going. This was one area of the race where I might say I beat most people, and that was with nutrition.

The need to eat is all-encompassing. But sadly, the desire to eat when in this state is non-existent. With horrific body fatigue, nothing sounded like it would be good to eat. I had to force myself to consume calories, and that's exactly how I looked at it. Calories had to go in, or out of the race I would go.

To continue, I had to pluck my log out of the swamp. On went the goggles and into the pond I dove to retrieve my submarine. I swam around the bottom for a while, found the only log lodged there, and assumed it had to be mine. The only problem was that with that hideous log, I couldn't swim back to the surface. It was so heavy that it anchored me to the bottom. Swimming back up without my log seemed like a bad idea, as I did not know if I could find it again. Walking out seemed like the only option, so that's what I did.

Back on dry land, I noticed there were a *lot* of people crowded along the shoreline looking into the mud with very concerned looks on their faces. Christian looked ready to dive in. I asked what they were all looking at, and Christian, with relief, exclaimed that I had been under for three minutes. They all thought I was dead. I guess it took a lot longer to find that log than I had thought.

As if being stuck in the swamp was not bad enough, I was ordered to climb under the highway through a one-hundred-metre storm culvert half filled with water. There was just enough room in the culvert to crawl on my belly and keep my head above the water. The organizers even offered to tie a rope to our feet so they could pull us out if we panicked in the tunnel. There were a few competitors with claustrophobia that prevented them from doing this task.

It was in the middle of that tube where I fully understood that I too had an issue. I froze. Not due to cold, but due to an overwhelming sense of panic and anxiety. I was on my belly in a two-foot-diameter drainage pipe, and I was halfway under the highway. I had a backpack that got caught on every inch of the rusty pipe, and I was trying to push a water-soaked log. At some points I was completely stuck. Flashes of being trapped inside a flaming helicopter burned through my eyes, and my whole body seized.

That was all bad.

I'd known that random events would trigger bursts like this, but I had been sure I had it all under control. Apparently, I was wrong. I knew I had to get out of the tunnel or I was going to need a rescue, and I do not think I could ever have lived that down. Was pride going to be my downfall?

I stared at the end of the tunnel and looked only at the light, as that was where I had to be. Pounding the log in front of me, I pulled my pack along like a dead body. My eyes never left the light at the end of the tunnel. Slowly, progress was being made. My heart felt like it was going to explode out of my chest as I put every piece of my strength into this task. Push, drag, stare at the light. Push, drag, stare at the light. As I got close and closer to the end of the tunnel, I realized that this was the crux of the race for me, and anything I had to do after this would be a cakewalk compared to the terror in the tunnel.

I poked my head out of the tunnel and lay upside down in the drainage water while sucking in glorious fresh air. I had lived. Apparently, I still had some demons in my closet, but those could be dealt with later. It was now time to get as far from that tunnel as possible.

We were tasked to go up the other side of the valley with our logs and packs, and into the rain. It was almost dark. The rain had started at around three p.m. The slope was about 2000 vertical feet of the most horrendous routing possible—almost none of it on any existing trails. It was pure bushwhacking through stinging nettles. By that point in the race, my legs were a mass of cuts, scratches, and open wounds. That just meant that every inch of forward movement through the fields of stinging nettles felt like a blowtorch was being applied to my legs. The beauty of having massive amounts of stinging nettle cuts is that the pain stays with you for at least forty-eight hours. That's the gift that keeps on giving. But my memory of the tunnel still lingered in the back of my head, and I decided that stinging nettle was a vacation in comparison.

This, though, was where I found my new friend PJ Rakowski. He happened to be walking with me up the side of the mountain and we stuck together from then on. PJ was dragging his log on a rope while I carried mine on my pack. From that point forward, all pain and suffering was being shared, and we turned it into laughter and entertainment.

The stinging nettle wasn't all that bad compared to the last 400 vertical feet, where barbed wire was strung over the trail about eighteen inches off the ground. The trail was intensely steep. It was pouring, and I had a fifty-pound pack and a fifty-pound log to get up the hill under the barbed wire. It was only 300 metres of trail, yet it took us over an hour and a half to do it, and I thought we were going fast. There was a massive river of mud coming down the trail at me the entire time. I had mud in every crack and orifice of my body and a few more.

The best thing about it was knowing I was not alone in this. Everyone else would run into the same shit storm as I was in, and they would not be laughing and enjoying it. The scars down my back from all the barbs cutting me on that section are a great reminder of a fun night in the rain.

On several occasions while assaulting the barbed wire, PJ and I stood up and discussed the need to finish this task. Why not just step out of the barbed wire and walk around the obstacle? Who was there to watch us, and what would they do about it? It was two a.m., pitch black, and thundering down rain.

We decided that we would know, and we would not be able to live with ourselves if we were to do something like that. So back into the mud we dropped and up the hill we battled.

The checkpoint was only a few hundred metres beyond the barbed wire, where our bib numbers were marked down, and we were told to go back to the farm by the same path we had taken to get up. PJ and I laughed hysterically, knowing that we would see the barbed wire again in a few minutes.

By midnight I made it back to the farm. The river was now twelve feet deep, and a raging Class IV rapid of mud and trees. My greatest concern was that we would be sent back to the Apostle Hell in cold water, and I did not know if I had it in me to go through hypothermia again. I was sure the organizers would do this, as it is what I would have done to get everyone to quit. Apparently, they are much nicer than I am.

FINDING JOY IN THE PAIN

It was time to chop firewood and I was in heaven. You see, I chop firewood for fun and exercise at home. I know how,

and I'm damn good at it and consider it very relaxing to do. There is a certain catharsis to the physically violent act of bringing the axe down to split wood, combined with the tangible accomplishment as one stack gets smaller and the other bigger. Also, I'd brought a mean splitting axe with me, honed to a razor-sharp instrument of forest death.

At that point, I had no idea what place I was in the race and didn't care. I was alive, drinking a beer, chopping wood in the dark, loving every minute of it, and still in the game.

Beer in the middle of a race may sound ridiculous to most, but when you are physically exhausted and questioning your sanity, then anything that boosts your mental state is good. A cold beer had that effect on me. That and Christian was having a beer, and I didn't want him to look silly drinking alone at four a.m.

Many components of the Death Race were, coincidentally, community service projects. At that moment, I was helping buck the winter supply of firewood for the town. I chopped four cords of wood (pack off, log down). Just enough to fill the box of an eight-foot pickup truck, four times over. Easy. Three hours later, and I was almost caught back up to the leaders.

I choked down another buttered burger glued with almond butter, and I was off and heading up the trail. The organizers let us dump our logs, just to be instructed to fill up our five-gallon pail with water. I was told to follow the trail up the mountainside to the next checkpoint, and if I had spilled any more than one inch of water out of the bucket, I'd have to come back down and refill. Off I went.

Twenty yards away—and out of sight—I took off my Gore-Tex jacket, used the rope I'd brought, and tied the jacket on as a lid. No water was going to be coming out of my bucket. I heard later that some people had asked if they could use a lid and were strictly told there were no lids allowed. Fortunately, I was smart enough not to ask that question. Score number one for the suddenly-and-somewhat-redeemed-smart guy. I also made sure I had a full bladder, just in case I needed to top up the bucket before the next checkpoint.

The following three hours went like this: walk ten steps, put the bucket down, and change hands. Pick up the bucket and walk ten steps, put the bucket down and change hands. I did that for five kilometres and up 2000 vertical feet. A miserable hell is a gross understatement. By this point, I was just running on pure mental fortitude. The muscles had given up long ago. Every body part was beyond hurting, the blisters were huge...but I was endorphin-driven happy and therefore anything was possible.

This task manifested itself to test the limits of my endurance both physically and mentally. I've always known I should be able to endure moments in life like this, and it was looking like I was getting my wish. Be careful what you ask for, as you may just get it.

At the checkpoint, the water level was measured and found to be acceptable, then they pushed my bucket over and dumped the water out. I smiled like I had just won the lottery. They asked if I was annoyed that they had just dumped out the water and that I had carried it up there for nothing. It was thought that this should frustrate the competitors, but for me it had the opposite effect. The bucket was empty, and I did not need to carry it any farther.

Task completed, I looped back to the farm and was told I was in fifth place. At four p.m.—a full forty-eight hours after this had begun—there was a mandatory meeting at the church. It was only ten a.m. Still lots of mental torture to go.

To continue with the community-service aspect of the race, we were sent up the road to plant vegetables at another farm. This really did make me feel like a chump for having paid a $300 entry fee to do all the work in Pittsfield.

With vegetables in the ground, we had to return to the starting-point farm. The instructions were to make our way back down the river. It had calmed slightly from the raging torrent of the night before but was still moving swiftly enough that there was a zero-percent chance of walking within it. Behind the barn where I was planting, I just happened to spot an old inner tube. Score another one for being crafty, sneaky, and having a world of ingenuity. Off I went floating down the river in my tube, laughing the whole way. I smiled triumphantly when I passed the woman who was in fourth place. One more lesson in the world of getting the job done and not asking how they want it done.

It was then I was given a choice. I could say that the race was done for me, or I could go back to the opposite side of the valley and hit the checkpoint at the top. The day previous, that route had taken me six hours, and it involved the barbed-wire obstacle from hell. Realizing that the meeting at the church was in two hours, I decided to go get a front-row seat and wait. Of all things, the organizers said that was a wise choice and congratulated me on the event. I was utterly confused now, as I was sure I was being set up for failure but couldn't figure out how.

The woman I had passed in the river chose to head up the other side of the mountain. Nobody knows why, but it really was a herculean effort on her part to do so. Eventually, the organizers tracked her down on the hillside and brought her back to the church. They'd never expected anyone to actually do it.

At church, it was announced that the race was over. I figured that was the way it would be, with racers stretched all over the mountains. Organizers had no idea where anyone was anymore. One guy that was missing from the day before arrived back in town by hitchhiking. He had ended up ten miles downstream after he got lost in the middle of the night.

I earned fourth place, and my prize was a two-dollar plastic skull that read "Finisher" on it. This remains one of my most prized possessions. There are few prizes in life I have put so much blood, sweat, and tears into achieving.

On the drive home, Christian asked me if I thought that I might have been able to win the race. Damn, I had never even thought about that. All I wanted to do was to see if I could finish. Now I knew I was more than capable.

Suddenly, all I was thinking about was how I wanted to return and win. I was immediately planning how I would adjust my training, my nutrition, and what I'd have to do to prepare in order to champion it the next year. Christian agreed to be my support guy again, and I was signed up for the next year before I got home. I was going to win.

GROWING UP IN CALGARY

I WAS BORN IN CALGARY, ALBERTA, IN 1970, THE YOUNGEST of three.

Dad was a geologist and Mom took on the full-time job of raising a trio of full-throttle children while simultaneously being an active community volunteer. Being the youngest, I had to learn everything quickly, or I was going to be left behind.

My dad ran the hockey program for the Elbow Park Community where we lived. Playing hockey formed an integral part of my formative years.

Beside the hockey rink was a massive sledding hill. This meant that every spare minute of our winter months was either spent playing hockey or hiking up the sledding hill, pulling our toboggans. I look back and recognize this to be the foundation of all my athletic prowess.

Mom dropped us off at the hockey rink after breakfast so we could play all day. We would walk the six blocks home, stop in for lunch, get a drink, and grab the toboggan. Dad picked us up later when dinner was ready. This was what happened every weekend of the winter.

Yes, we had a TV, but it was black and white, with only three channels and more static than a picture. Video games consisted of the first generation of the Atari 2600, and Asteroids was the high-end game of the time. I got to grow up knowing that the save icon was a floppy disk and you needed twenty-two of them to load any program onto a Commodore 64.

The summers were equally filled with activity. Our activities were extreme. My friends and I owned a sense of adventure, BMX bikes, and had no limitations as to where we could or would not go.

With thirty-five cents in our pockets, we were rich beyond belief. Off we would ride on our bikes for the day's adventure. Nobody ever had a plan, as it just unfolded organically along the way. Thirty-five cents was the budget. Ten cents to call home to find out when dinner was, (the only real rule we had,) and the remaining twenty-five cents was to buy a Slurpee and a bag of salt-and-vinegar chips. This was our fuel for the day. If we needed water, we just stopped at some stranger's house, ran up, and drank from the hose. Nobody carried a water bottle, and helmets were unheard of. It was just what one did. This was normal.

By the end of a summer riding BMX bikes fifty kilometres a day, we were all in phenomenal physical condition and ready for hockey.

My mom signed me up for swim lessons in the spring, soccer in the fall...and hockey in the winter was always a given. On most Sundays we went skiing near Banff.

Dad provided some of the best motivation a kid could want, strictly by how much he cared about hockey in our community. He oversaw two outdoor hockey rinks, which meant that he did everything from putting up the boards in the fall, to scraping the ice and flooding it nightly at -30°. He rarely asked for help and was commonly heard telling the young kids that if you don't use your muscles, you'll get old and die. He was usually saying that while running a snowblower at night, no hat on, with a smoke hanging out the corner of his mouth. Hockey was his life, and he put more than one hundred percent effort into it. I was constantly inspired by that devotion to the sport.

Dad also made sure there were plenty of double-wide steel shovels to scrape the ice with. We did not have a Zamboni, so the rink needed to be scraped by hand before my dad could flood it each night. These shovels needed two kids to push them, and even then, it was a daunting task. Nobody got away with playing hockey on these rinks without scraping the ice after. This is what developed the monster-sized legs that helped me through life.

I grew up doing the Nancy Greene ski league at Fortress Mountain, AB. Every Sunday I skied with the same group of kids and a coach, and sometime during the day we would race against another team. By the time I was twelve, I won every race of the year, as well as the provincial finals. Our team was top in the province.

My mom took on the job of raising three rambunctious kids involved in every sport imaginable. She did this while volunteering at the "Next to New Shop," which was more like a high-end Salvation Army than anything else. My mother grew up as a ski racer and has an endless array of ski racing stories with Nancy Green and every other National Team ski racer for the past thirty years. Mom showed me what determination and hard work were by being the chief gatekeeper for all the downhill skiing events in the 1988 Olympics. This volunteer job took her four years to prep for and came off with Swiss-like precision. She has always been a cornerstone of the ski racing world in Alberta.

Since my dad organized the community hockey programs and did the scheduling, my team's hockey games were always late on Sunday night. This meant I could come back from the ski hill and squeeze in a hockey game. I have very fond memories of sleeping in the footwell of the family station wagon on the drive home. At least that was safer than sleeping in the back window of the car like my brother did.

As far as I could tell, my youth was one giant bout of physical exercise. My childhood activities prepared me for my future life of athletics.

Our family made a lot of sacrifices in order to be able to put three kids through hockey and ski racing. Most everything I used in sports was from the Sport Swap. Old stuff went back, and not-as-old stuff came out. These sacrifices were made so that our family could have a cabin in the mountains outside of Canmore, Alberta. My dad built the cabin the year I was born, and that was where we developed more of our leg strength. My dad would find a way to turn most things into great opportunities to exercise and build strength. The cabin had almost an acre of lawn to cut every weekend of the summer, and although there was an electric mower there, I was only allowed to use the push mower. With some story about not being old enough and a concern that I would cut off my toe, he constantly pushed the age that I could use the electric mower farther and farther down the road like dangling a carrot in front of a donkey. The lawn was mostly hill, the grass was always overgrown, and we had to get it cut before we were allowed to head down the creek to go rock hopping for the day.

In 1984, I discovered snowboarding.

The snowboard addiction stuck like Krazy Glue. That was the end of ski racing for me, and it was my foray into my first professional sport. Every winter day possible that I wasn't playing hockey, I was snowboarding. Sunshine Village and Fortress Mountain were the hills of choice at the time. Back then, they were also the only ski hills that allowed snowboarding.

Then, when I was sixteen, Dad decided that was the year I was going to build some serious strength, as I was going to stock the wood pile for the cabin. Alone. My brother went out with the family station wagon, chopped down the trees, and brought them back for me. I had the pleasure of sawing them into eighteen-inch lengths with a monster-sized swede saw, and then bucking them up with one of the most dismal axes known to man. This took me most of the summer to complete, and I never really appreciated the skills this gave me until I was in the Death Race and chopping firewood. Twenty years later, I found out that my brother had cut down the greenest, wettest, most knot-infested trees he could find. Watching me fight through that pile of horrific wood had made him smile with delight. What more could one ask for in a brother?

When grade twelve came to an end, it was off to university for me. I graduated high school at eighteen and was accepted into Simon Fraser University in Vancouver, BC. It was a real toss-up for me, as all my other friends from Sunshine Village had just moved out to Whistler, and they were living the dream as snowboarders. Yet, there I was, sitting in school trying to become an engineer.

University lasted all of one semester for me. The academic probation letter had my name written all over it. I had spent every weekend up at Whistler, snowboarding and mountain biking, and apparently had done scant studying. The road to becoming an engineer veered off a cliff.

I packed up my dorm room and moved to Whistler. School would always be there if or when I wanted to go back. I had the opportunity to be a pro-snowboarder, and I went for it.

From there, the story of my life is one very long series of episodes of successes, injuries, recoveries, and dream chasing. Upon reflection of what I achieved, and how I miraculously got to where I am today, I would say it all came down to one thing: I seized every opportunity that came my way. No matter how big the challenge was, I kept taking the opportunities that were offered. Every link, in the chain of events of my life, has been full of potential. I have no regrets.

BECOMING A SKI GUIDE

I HAVE SAID THAT MY ACCOMPLISHMENTS IN LIFE HAVE come from taking advantage of the opportunities that were presented to me. This is exactly how I started my life as a ski guide.

During the winter of 1988-89, Ken Achenbach convinced me to go heli-skiing for a week at Mike Wiegele Heli-Skiing in the Cariboo Mountains of BC. He told me it would be the most fun I ever had, and his persuasiveness convinced me in short order that I would be missing out on life if I was to turn it down. Not to be one to turn down a fun opportunity, I booked myself in.

On my drive from Whistler to Blue River, it dawned on me that this trip was making me broke. I'd spent every penny I had on the week of heli-skiing, and I had fifty dollars left to get me back to Whistler and figure out how to eat. But I figured that life would sort itself out the same as it always had before.

Upon arrival at the lodge, the front desk girl greeted me by name as I walked in the door. How could this possibly be? This was impossible. Looking back on it, maybe it was easier than I would have thought. I was eighteen years old, I'd arrived in a fifty-dollar car, and I was dressed in jeans and a dirty t-shirt. I probably looked a wee bit different than the normal fifty-year-old wealthy guests they usually catered to. We were the first of the snowboard guests, and I'm pretty sure we fit the perceived image of snowboarding perfectly.

I met Mike Wiegele the first night at dinner, and he treated Ken and me like any other guest in the house. Mike was the single most excited person I had ever met in the snow and skiing industry. He had an endless barrage of questions about snowboarding and was beside himself with excitement about taking us in his group the following day.

After my first run, I remember thinking that I would have to go home and make more money, because I was sure as hell going to be doing this again. One run and I was hooked. I was addicted to the white powder, and it was expensive.

That week of snowboarding led to us going again at Christmastime with a much larger group of snowboarders. Boxing Day was a slow time for Mike, so we would bring twenty snowboarders with us and ride for two days at a screaming good discount.

Ken and I were hooked on Wiegle's and figured there had to be a way to go there without paying. That's when we realized that our friends who ran the snowboard magazines would probably want to do a story on Wiegle's. Ken took the photos, our friend Colin Whyte did the writing, and I was the stunt monkey. Over the following three years we did at least five trips there, making stories for every snowboard magazine in the world. In short order, the place became known as Wiegele World.

The multiple visits to Wiegele's caught the attention of one of the guests, Tom Pfleger. He wanted to learn to snowboard, so he invited me, Ken, and our friend Craig Kelly, who would arguably become the most influential snowboarder ever. When the front desk staff called me and told me that a guest wanted to bring me up for a week of heli-skiing so that I could teach him how to snowboard, I first thought it was a gag and I was being set up. They assured me it was not, and that I should say yes as this was an opportunity not to be missed.

In short order, the teaching led to going to Wiegele's for four weeks a year and sometimes more. We taught Tom and all his friends how to snowboard, which is how I ended up teaching Gerry Lopez, Laird Hamilton, and Derek Doerner, who were the top big-wave surfers in the world.

I remember the first night at dinner when I met the surfing crew from Hawaii. Ken Achenbach and I rolled up to the table and introductions were made all around. Then Gerry and Laird said how excited and honoured they were to meet us. My eyeballs were spinning around in my head as I tried to come to grips with the Hawaiian legends being stoked to meet us. We were the dirtbag snowboarders, and they were the top surfers in the world. But it slowly dawned on me that we were in my world of snow, helicopters, and snowboarding and not at the beach. To them, I assume it meant they were meeting people that were the top in a sport mostly new to them, and we were the legends.

One of the best side bonuses of meeting the Hawaiians was going surfing with them at Tavarua in Fiji. They had just started the tow-in surfing, and these guys were leading the world with it. Tom had invited us all to go surfing together so we could experience their world like they had come snowboarding with us. Off to Tavarua we went, having no idea at all what we were getting into. I am a decent surfer but being pinned to the bottom of the ocean by a massive wave scares the daylights out of me.

That led me to hanging onto the tow rope attached to the back of the jet ski, while Jerry Lopez towed me into a massive (in my opinion) wave at a surf break called Cloudbreak. This break is just a small reef in the middle of the ocean, ten kilometres from the island of Tavarua, yet we could see the foaming spray from the waves at that distance without binoculars.

Jerry looked over his shoulder and yelled at me to let go of the rope, as I was in the perfect position on the wave. I looked over my shoulder at the twenty-foot-tall wave crashing down behind me like a raging avalanche of death and yelled, "NO NO NO NO! GO GO GO!"

Lucky for me, Jerry went around but was confused as to why I didn't let go, since I'd been set up perfectly. "Set up perfectly for my funeral," I replied. I told him I needed the smallest wave he could find and not the biggest. Maybe I shouldn't have pushed him so hard to jump off thirty-foot cliffs at Wiegele's.

The next wave I rode was much friendlier, right up until I became mesmerized by the fish and sea life that were in the wall of the crystal-clear water on the face of the wave. That was when the top of the wave slapped me upside the head and pummeled me right onto the reef. And there I was, stuck on the inside of the reef, staring at massive waves, and completely lacking the skill set to paddle back through them to the boat that we came in on. Fortunately for me, Derek Doerner, who was also the top lifeguard in the world, showed up on another jet ski and saved my sorry butt.

After explaining what had happened, what I saw, and how I got stuck on the reef, they all exclaimed that I had been barreled, and that was exactly what happens to everyone the first time in a barrel. After that day I decided that the small waves were more my thing and that maybe paddling into the big waves might be something I should learn before towing into places I figured I ought not to be on my own. For the rest of that day, I sat on the boat and had a front row seat to the greatest surfing legends in the world working their magic in huge surf. This will never be forgotten.

By the time 1994 came around, I was thinking about going back to university, and I had all the course books lined up for financial management. It was time in my life to grow up and become an adult. That was when the next big life-opportunity presented itself.

While I was talking with Mike one night, he asked me if I had thought about becoming a guide. I had always looked up to ski guides as gods, and never really thought that I could attain that level. I mentioned that I was going back to university and was going to study financial management. He gave me the look that he usually reserved for cats, and he said that I should become a guide, as he had a job for me. His words were, "You are a pain in the ass as a guest, and you know the runs better than my guides, so why don't you work here?"

My jaw hit the floor, and I mumbled incoherently for a few minutes as my brain came to grips with the fact that the financial management plan had just gotten tossed out the window. I now knew I was going to be a guide. I hugged Mike and walked away in a daze as I had just been offered the job of a lifetime. I didn't have any of the skills for it yet, but why should that stop me? Like everything in my life, the details would sort themselves out on their own.

Two months later, and I was on the Canadian Ski Guide Association (CSGA) Level I course in Blue River. Bob Sayer, our guide for the past four years, was my instructor. Some days of the course seemed like we were on Bob's crazy mountain adventure tour. I believe those adventures were the cornerstone to my guiding and learning. He made the training incredibly challenging, yet totally unforgettable. Navigating the mountains with zero viability and hundred-kilometre winds ended up being enjoyed instead of feared. I could not imagine a better way to train as a guide. Bob was my main mentor in the guiding world and has been ever since.

The following winter I was on the guiding roster at Wiegele World and living an entirely new dream. Sure, I had been in a helicopter crash in 1990 that almost killed me, but why should that stop me from working in helicopters every day of the winter? I was twenty-four and still thought I was indestructible.

One portion of the guiding process was achieving my Level III Canadian Ski Instructors Alliance (CSIA) certification. The course would only require me to attain the Level II certification, but Mike Wiegele said that to work for him, I needed my Level III. Seeing as it was his company I was going to work for, I set out to pass the Level III course. Few instructors will obtain their Level III, as it generally takes many years of training, mentorship, and an incredible amount of on-hill teaching to be ready for the exam.

I was taking the exam with a fellow guide, and over the course of the winter we had only skied in powder snow. We had worn thirty-pound backpacks and had not taught a single lesson at a ski resort. What we *had* done was guide every day of the winter while taking guests safely out in the mountains and helping them with their powder-skiing technique. Slightly different, but still all the same thing in our minds.

On day one of the course, our instructors had a serious chat at the end of the day and told us that if we were normal ski instructors, they would tell us to go home and cut our losses, as there was no way we would pass the course. Our technique was not up to their standard, and there was no way we could correct it over the week of the course. They did give us the benefit of the doubt since we had only skied powder and had always had on heavy backpacks. The examiners said they would give us a chance, but they really did not have much hope for our success. This was probably the best news we could have received, as it gave us the motivation we needed and added a little extra challenge to the course.

We had contacts within the Ski Patrol, so we went up the lifts early each day to work on our technique and refine our skills as the course required. We finished each day sitting on the back of the truck in the parking lot while enjoying a six-pack of beer. That was when we were asked to give a talk on professionalism during the evening class, since we were respected members of the mountain guide community. We stared at the empty beer cans, shrugged our shoulders, and said of course we would be happy to give a talk on professionalism. After the examiner left, I looked at the beer in my hand, stared at my friend, and before I could say anything he said, "This is a talk on professionalism, not hypocrisy. No problem." We laughed our way through the whole evening and did a fantastic job on our presentation.

The final skiing exam day arrived, and so did two feet of new snow. While the rest of the students looked terrified about having to ski powder after a week of skiing on rock-hard snow, I thought that it was going to be the secret to my success. At the start of the exam, I offered to go first and said that I would be teaching how to ski through soft, powdery moguls. I passed with flying colours, and I knew whatever snow gods were out there, they loved me.

Over the following seven years, I progressed through my guiding and snow science courses. The CSGA is a mentorship program where most of the experience gained is with on-the-job training while being supervised by more senior guides. It is an amazing system where you get to work in the industry you are training for while obtaining real-life experience. I remember one of the days of my Level III exam where I was out on an all-day ski tour in some of the most savage weather conditions I had ever experienced. We made a radio call back to the ski lodge at one point to give them a weather update from the top of the mountain. It went something like this: "The wind is blowing anywhere between eighty and a hundred and twenty kilometres. The visibility ranges from six to eight feet, and the temperature is close to -20°C. It is beautiful out here." This was the summation of seven years of hard training under the supervision of Bob Sayer. I am eternally grateful for his mentorship and how much fun he made traipsing about in the mountains.

That spring I passed my Level III CSGA and obtained the title of lead guide. This meant that I was entitled to run my own operation and could take my own helicopter out unsupervised. At times this was hard to comprehend, as I took out a five-million-dollar helicopter with ten people and was allowed to go anywhere I wanted. The ski area was as big as Switzerland. I was constantly in awe that I had achieved this position and responsibility.

It's great being the guide and going down the run first each time.
Photo: Michaela Chroustova

One day, a doctor was telling me how much responsibility he had, and how if he made a mistake, someone died. I recall laughing and saying, "Big deal!" He gave me a very inquisitive look and once again told me how much pressure he was under to not make a mistake. I told him that if I made a mistake that day, I could kill thirty-seven people and destroy a five-million-dollar helicopter, and that maybe there was just a wee bit of pressure on me too. This is something that I keep in mind every day that I go out in the mountains.

During my first few years at Wiegele World, my scars were still quite new, and very red. Most guests knew about the helicopter crash but did not know I was one of the survivors. I recall one group I was skiing with who were certainly questioning their new young guide who had all the scars. At dinner the first night I told them that I had been in the helicopter crash and several friends had died, but I had dealt with all my demons and was ok to be back in helicopters. Then I said that I was safer to be with than anyone else, because really, what were the odds that I would be in another crash? Apparently this made a big impression, because I was suddenly accepted into the group. I was one of them.

I really did have a life that was as good as it could get. I got paid to go skiing all winter long, while being fed every evening by world-renowned chefs.

The summers would have me moving back to Whistler, where mountain biking and travelling consumed my life.

All of that because I kept taking advantage of the opportunities presented to me.

HOW I MET MY WIFE

FOR THIRTEEN YEARS I WORKED AS A GUIDE IN THE TOWN of Blue River, British Columbia. With a population of 350 people, one gas station, and a small liquor-cum-grocery store, it was largely viewed as a highway pit-stop. A place you passed through.

For the first five years I worked for Wiegele's, I lived over top of the gas pumps at the local motel. While it may not have been classy, it did have the most amazing views of the Monashee Mountains. The 200-metre walk to work in the morning was dazzling.

Wiegele was known as a very generous man within the community of Blue River. As part of his devotion to the town, he took the local school kids out heli-skiing every Saturday. In 1998, at age twenty-eight, I was given the job as the lead guide in charge of the school program. Some of the students were beginners and some were talented, experienced snowboarders. My job was to create a fabulous experience for everyone.

I found myself helping to build a large jump on the side of the mountain with one of the local teenagers. He wanted to learn how to do a backflip, and I was hoping to impress the teacher leading his school group. The teacher's name was Lee Erickson, and I was willing to try anything to catch her eye.

Lee brought the school group each weekend, and I was always impressed with how thoughtful and caring she was with the students. She shepherded them like they were all kids of her own. This was amazing. I just had to figure out a way to find more time to talk with her.

There I was, teaching several kids who were first-timers on skis and hiking up and down the hill doing backflips with one of the older boys. If this was not enough to get her attention, I didn't know what would be. Funnily enough, years later I would find out that it was the care and concern I expressed for one of the younger kids learning how to ski for the first time that had caught her eye. She thought my backflips were just showing off. She was right.

Partway through that winter, I left Blue River to go to New Mexico to teach skiing for two months as part of gaining further guiding credentials. This meant that any chance I had to get to know Lee was at an end. When I returned, the winter season would be over.

Fortunately, upon my return to Blue River in the spring, there was a year-end Snow Blowers Ball at the local community hall. I was certain Lee would be there, and I dressed to impress. I found myself nervous, like a teenager going to my first high school dance. What was it in this woman that made me feel like that? I had only gone skiing with her a few times, during which I only had the chance to talk with her for minutes, but I was giddy and love-struck.

At the dance, I saw Lee across the room. Our eyes met, and I knew this was my moment. I winked at her. To my astonishment, she turned around and walked away.

I went home deflated and thinking that maybe my scars were a stumbling block in my romantic life, and that any dream of a life with a beautiful woman was slowly fading out.

What I did not find out until years later was that Lee was so impressed I had winked at her, that she had spun around to tell her friend about the cute guide who'd winked at her...he was back. Lee saw beyond the scars. Apparently, her friend asked what Lee had done in response, and much to her horror, she realized that she had just turned around and walked away. We can laugh at this now.

After five years of living in Blue River, I realized that if I was going to continue with the career of a heli-ski guide, then I needed my own house. Preferably one that would also double as a great socializing location for my friends. While the skiing there is the best in the world, it just isn't that enjoyable to hang out in old motel rooms at night.

I bought a piece of bare land in town in the middle of the winter, and I started construction on my house that spring. It was just 500 metres down the road from where Lee was living. Despite what had happened at the Snow Blower's Ball, I had convinced myself that some way, somehow, we would end up dating. I was just missing the plan for how that was going to happen. Then, like everything else in my life, the opportunity presented itself.

Every day at three-thirty, Lee went out for a run and would just happen to run by my construction site. And, as shocking as it may seem, I coincidentally managed to be at the front of the lot at the same time, doing some kind of work. We began to chat every day. Little did I know she had changed her running route so she would pass by me every day. Love is a wonderful thing.

Every morning before school started, Lee and a fellow teacher went out mountain biking, and Lee invited me to join them one day. When the two arrived, I came out wearing a pink bathrobe, swim fins, goggles, and a mask. I thought this would be hilarious—I was met with blank stares. No laughing. No comments. Just the blank stares. Awkwardly, I went back in the house and changed into bike gear and off we went. No more words were said about the pink bathrobe. I really feared that maybe Lee didn't have a sense of humour at all. What I did not know was that as soon as I went back inside, they buckled over with laughter. They thought this was one of the funnier things they had ever seen. By the time I came back out, the laughing had stopped, and nothing was said. My joke had worked, but I had no idea. After all, it was five a.m.

Our first official date was when friends in town were having their wedding anniversary dinner. The wife had arranged that Lee and I would both be there for dinner and was secretly being a matchmaker. She knew we would be great together and was instrumental in helping us succeed. That night was our first kiss, and the start of an amazing new adventure in life.

I was constantly impressed with Lee and the fact that she saw right through my scars and accepted me as I was. For her, scars don't define who a person is. I found that people like this really were very rare. Especially very attractive women such as Lee. I felt like I had won the lottery and was floating on cloud nine.

Dinner with my gorgeous wife, Lee. Photo: Lydia Schwartz

After four years of dating, Lee mentioned something about wanting to have kids soon, and that I needed to decide in the near term if I was going to be there or not. Hints were being dropped all the time, such as: "Why don't we go ring shopping today?" Or: "How many kids do you want to have? I'd like five." I was smart enough to take the hint seriously and had an engagement ring made.

Deciding when and where to ask Lee to marry me was a daunting task. Did I take her heli-skiing and ask on the top of the mountain? In the boat while barefoot waterskiing? In the forest while running? Eventually I decided to ask her while skating on an outdoor lake at the Jasper Park Lodge, in Jasper,

BC. Thankfully she said yes. A happier moment in my life I cannot remember.

A year later we were married and living in the house I had built in Blue River. With our first child on the way, we decided to move back to Whistler. More opportunities had arrived in life, and it was time to take advantage of them.

The chance to buy into Powder Mountain Catskiing[1] appeared. I just could not turn it down. This was the opportunity to run my own business, be a guide, and raise our forthcoming child in the greatest ski town on the planet. Opportunity was knocking again, and we were opening the door.

1　Catskiing is guided backcountry skiing in which the skiers are transported up the mountain in a snowcat, a grooming machine with a cabin on the back.

MY LIFE OF SNOWBOARDING

THE ADVENT OF SNOWBOARDING IN MY LIFE SET EVERY-thing else in motion.

It was 1984 and I was fourteen years old. While watching a Warren Miller film in Calgary, I saw a snowboarder for the first time on the big screen. Warren Miller is known as one of the godfathers of the ski-movie industry, and snowboarding just wasn't heard of back then. I was captivated.

I had never seen a snowboard or a snowboarder in real life. Nor had I talked to anyone who had ever attempted it. All those things were irrelevant, as I was so magnetically drawn to the sport. It was all I talked about for weeks and weeks. My parents were sick of hearing about it, especially since I was a ski racer, my sister was a ski racer, and my mom was a ski racer. Between skiing and hockey, there was little time, if any, left for something as frivolous and unknown as snowboarding, in their eyes. But not mine...

I learned that there just happened to be a small start-up in Calgary that was trying to promote these burgeoning boards. When my parents went out of town for a few days, I skipped school, took my money, and went to The Snoboard Shop. I left with a new snowboard in hand, the happiest kid in the world. My parents still thought—and possibly hoped—it would just be a one-week fad and soon done with.

I went to Sunshine Village for my first day. Being fourteen years old and subsisting entirely on hockey and skiing, I was in great physical shape, and I thought I was quite a talented athlete. The guy in the ski movie made it look like anyone could do it!

The snowboard I started on looked nothing like the snowboards you see today. It had no metal edges, but it did have a couple of big metal fins on the sides near the back. These were supposedly to help you track straight while going down the hill. The fins would be a total hindrance to turning on hard-packed snow, but beggars can't be choosers.

The bindings were rudimentary plastic plates and a couple of nylon straps with fast-ex buckles. These were impossible to tighten over my boots. Oh, the boots! These were just plain old winter boots with a felt liner in them. They had about the same support as a pair of high-top runners.

Assuming I was going to carve it up just like the guy in the movie, I strapped myself in at the top of the ski lift and took off down the mountain. Reality was a very different story.

I went straight for about thirty metres and then when I leaned over to make a turn, the board stayed completely straight. The metal tracking fins were doing their job perfectly. I put more force into it, and the board immediately spun sideways, the downhill edge hooked in the snow, and I was thrown over onto my back so fast that it was like someone had kicked my feet out from under me. After my back hit the snow, my head whipped back and impacted so hard that all I could do was lie there and watch the funny-coloured stars spin around while my lungs were gasping for air. I looked like a guppy out of water.

Maybe snowboarding was a little harder than it looked? My fourteen-year-old self was a whole lot cockier than perhaps he should have been. I was, continually, being humbled by life.

By the end of the day, I did manage to get better control over the board. I was crashing less and less, but I stopped counting after about 200 falls. Every single muscle from my toes to my ears had been put through the wringer. I knew I would pay the price the next day.

The following weekend I felt like a seasoned pro, and only fell fifty times. I was most happy about not hooking the edge of the board and taking the backwards whiplash fall. I was making progress.

Needless to say, I was hooked. This sport was not going to be a passing fad, as I didn't even look at my skis for the rest of that year. My ski coach was not impressed. He was sure I had the talent to go a long way in racing. But it was my high school wrestling coach who was the most annoyed. I missed a wrestling tournament to go to a snowboard race. He'd been convinced that I'd be the city champ the next year. Snowboarding, however, worked out well for me after all.

The next year I went snowboarding every weekend of the winter. We would meet at Ken Achenbach's house in Calgary at six a.m. in order to get a ride to Sunshine Village to go snowboarding. This usually meant that we would show up at six, enter the house and wake up Ken and his brother, then wait for Ken to eat a bowl of Cheerios from a mug with the tiniest spoon known to man. This was a painful hell like no other. Eventually, though, we would depart in his VW van with AC/DC cranked so loud that there was no possibility for conversation.

This was an incredible time in sport for me, as we had nobody to learn anything from. Most days, I would be the only snowboarder on the mountain. If I wanted to learn a new trick, then I pretty much had to invent it. Skateboarding tricks were being adapted to snowboarding, while other moves were just made up along the way. This was as grassroots as the sport could ever get.

In 1986, the North American Championships were held at Sunshine Village, and I signed up. Apparently, every top snowboarder in the world was going to be there, and it was time to meet all the people I had only ever heard of.

The event was everything I had hoped and thought it could and would be. The half-pipe event was entirely new to me and taught us huge respect for those that could ride it. Terry Kidwell showed up on a snowboard that had a rounded tail and could go backwards. Jose Fernandez came in from Switzerland and gave us all a lesson in how to do backflips. My mind was blown.

After witnessing the top riders in the world, I was filled with a whole new level of stoke. Suddenly every trick had to be tried. Nothing was too far-fetched to attempt or make up. Everything seemed possible.

The following winter, I taught myself how to do a front flip, a backflip, and a McFlippy (a McTwist in skateboarding). This is going up the wall of the half-pipe and doing a front flip with a 540-degree spin. Mostly it looks like someone threw a cat out the window and somehow it landed on its feet.

To learn some of these tricks, we had to do it strictly by trial and error. There was nobody to copy from, and all we had was an idea and the motivation to try. Having never seen a McTwist before, I really didn't know what I was trying to achieve, but at seventeen years old I had no fear of trying. That was a point in life where there was little consequence to a fall, and rarely did it ever hurt the next day, no matter how many failures there were.

There was an amazing quarter-pipe in the back country of Sunshine Village that was fifteen feet tall and shaped perfectly by the wind. Many of us would spend our entire day there hiking up the hill, riding down, and trying new tricks on that quarter-pipe wall. Over and over and over. The McTwist was one of the better examples of that process.

I started out by trying a front summersault once I was airborne. But I quickly learned that when standing sideways on a snowboard, the body was not meant to just roll over forward, as I would just land on my ass and fall. I tried rotating my head and looking around to my right as I took off, and then over rotated, landed on my heels, and slammed my head into the snow. Finding the happy middle ground was the challenge. Eventually, though, I figured out to attack the quarter-pipe with more speed and wait until I was well up in the air before starting the front flip and adding the spinning rotation part way through the trick. This finally led to success after attempt number one hundred and twenty-four.

I signed up for the North American Championships in the amateur category in 1987. Again, all the top riders in the world showed up, and I was ready to see how my newfound skills would match up.

In the half-pipe event, I did a McTwist and ended my run with a massive front flip out the bottom of the pipe over the heads of the crowd. This of course put me in first place, and I walked home with a new mountain bike and a monster trophy of a bucking bronco.

The following year I signed up to compete as a pro. All the bigwigs from *Transworld Snowboard* and *International Snowboard* magazine were there. That meant the event would have coverage in the biggest of the snowboard periodicals. This was my opportunity.

During the winter that led up to the 1988 NorAms (North American competition), I knew I had to learn how to do a backflip. So far, my only experiences of doing backflips were on trampolines, and they had all ended up with the same horrific result of landing flat on the top of my head, where I was sure I had just broken my neck. My fear of backflips was all consuming, and I had not even tried one on a trampoline for at least ten years. Overcoming that fear seemed to be a necessity if I wanted to keep progressing.

A monster-sized freestyle jump was built in another back country area of Sunshine Village. The only thing to stop me from doing a backflip was fear and common sense. Luckily, at eighteen years old, it was easy to override those self-preservation instincts. I rode into the jump with way more speed than I needed with the mentality of "go big or go home" well entrenched in my mind. The jump was at least ten feet tall, so by the time I reached the top of it I was travelling almost vertically upwards. Up to this point, none of us had done a backflip, so the plan at this point was all hypothetical. The memory of Jose Fernandez from years previous was all I was going on.

The jump shot me at least ten more feet in the air, and as I was fully inverted while twenty feet in the air, I clearly remember thinking that I had no idea what to do next. So, I proceeded to freefall back to Planet Earth and plug into the snow on my head like a lawn dart— the exact same thing that had happened on the trampolines. Luckily, we had chosen an area where the landing was deep, fresh snow, and the only injury was a bruised ego and a dent in my pride.

I quickly figured out that to achieve success, looking up and backwards was what was needed. This would mean that my head would initiate the rotation, and if I kept my head rotating, the body would follow. This led to my second attempt at the back-flip...achieving total success. I may not have ridden away from the flip, but I at least landed on my board and not the top of my head. The following week, with one hundred more backflips in the bag, it was now my trick of choice. I could do a backflip off any little jump anywhere.

I was now ready for the next NorAm Championship.

The half-pipe event had a large jump leading into the run, and I took full advantage of that to use my new backflip skills to start my run. That was certainly a crowd pleaser.

The end of the weekend saw me standing on the podium with a first in the half-pipe, a first in the giant slalom, and second in the moguls. This also gave me the title of overall North American Snowboard Champion.

I was eighteen years old, a North American Champion, and I was now thick into the greatest sport in my life. I was living a dream that, just a few years previous, had seemed impossible. It felt like the world just allowed me to choose whatever life I wanted to live. The options were endless.

That spring I graduated from high school. As I've mentioned, I made a brief appearance at university, just in time to realize I wanted to be in Whistler a lot more than I wanted to be in school.

I packed all my worldly belongings into my car and drove to Whistler for the 1988/89 season. The original Snoboard Shop from Calgary had opened a new store there and had an accompanying house as well. If I was to help at the store, I could live in the attic of the house for free! This was an opportunity not to be turned down.

On any given weekend, that snowboard house could have up to twenty-five people living in it. My room was the attic, and I had to climb a ladder to access it. The high point of the ceiling was five feet, and I had to crawl around to avoid smacking my head. The squirrel lived on one side, and me on the other. We had a deal. He didn't eat my stuff, and I didn't put out any traps to catch him. We got along just fine.

It was normal to get up in the morning and find five people we had never seen before sleeping on the floor in the living room. When we asked who they were, and where they'd come from, the answer was usually that some common friend had said they could just go to Whistler and stay at the snowboard house. We would be cool with it. It was through times like this that we met our new best friends, and often we found ourselves sleeping on the floors of their houses around North America in the following years.

When the house was rented there had been a discussion about putting down a damage deposit. The response we got from the old Frenchman was: "Do not worry about it. Anything that can be broken, has already been broken." Apparently, he was right, although I think we did our best to out-party anything he had done.

One guy lived in an eight-foot-long hallway, others were in the basement, on couches, or under the stairs. The who's-who of the snowboard industry were living or spending time in that house. There were five cars valued at fifty dollars each parked in front. But everyone had a thousand-dollar mountain bike. A large yellow dog lived on the porch. The house was covered in snowboard company banners, and if that was not enough, the tour bus stopped in front every day to take pictures of the iconic house. It was the place to be. It was this life in Whistler that I wouldn't trade for anything else. We snowboarded all day, came home and watched *The Blues Brothers* on TV (again), and then would head out to the bar for a night of drinking and dancing, only to repeat the process again the next day. We were the exact stereotype of every baggy-panted snowboarder you have ever seen. Except I was the only guy who didn't wear the baggy pants. I still do not understand the desire to have one's pants hang down at the back of one's ass.

Though I called Whistler home, for several years I would pack my sports car and head out on the snowboard tour around North America. I drove wherever I could, trying to hit at least one event every weekend.

That was the point in snowboarding, where money flowed like water. It was the hot new sport and every company wanted in on the action. The skateboard and dirt bike industries were making inroads into the business, and sponsorship opportunities were everywhere. *Barfoot Snowboards* customized my own model of board, while other companies provided goggles, clothing, boots, gloves, and even Rubber Ducky Condoms. Yes, I was sponsored by a condom company. My parents were *not* impressed with this choice. My mom took my Rubber Ducky t-shirts and threw them in the trash.

On any given weekend, it was possible to win up to $10,000 in prize money, and I had a deal with my sponsors that they would match my contest winnings. This really was a license to print money. Having five additional sponsors meant that a big cash weekend was worth a lot of money.

The desire to continually push our limits led to me thinking about how to do a backflip with a 360. I watched the freestyle skiers do it, and it didn't look all that hard. Then again, any professional makes what they are doing look easy. My first attempt at this was while at a snowcat skiing operation in the interior of BC called Snow Much Fun Cat skiing. I built a large jump off the side of the cat road and had every belief in the world that I would make it on my first attempt. The backflip I had perfected already, so the idea of adding a full spin into the middle of the rotation seemed simple to me.

On my first attempt, I went straight up into the air, got halfway through the backflip, did none of the spin, and darted back into the snow on my head. It was the exact same result as my first attempt at the backflip. Luckily for me, it was into deep powder, and I did not break my neck. Attempt number two had a far better outcome. I thought more about the body mechanics of the trick and realized I needed to start the spin at the same time as the backflip rotation. This meant that all I needed to do was go up the jump and look over my left shoulder, and the rest of the trick should take care of itself. Shockingly enough, it worked perfectly. The second try had total success. This rapidly became a trick that I could do on almost any jump. For some reason, nobody else wanted to try that trick back in 1989, and for many years I was the only one doing it.

I was proud of all my accomplishments within the sport, and how many stories and photos that I had printed in the snowboard magazines, but there was one achievement I was most proud of. That was doing the first backflip in a mogul event in snowboarding.

The Ocean Pacific Pro Summer Surfout was a new event for the summer of 1989 on Blackcomb Mountain in Whistler. There was a half-pipe event, an obstacle course, and the moguls.

The obstacle course competition was on one of the foggier days on the mountain that I can remember. After competing in versions of this in California, where I excelled in this event, I was excited to be competing on my home turf. This version of the event included points for the tricks a person did on the jumps as well as how fast the course was completed. I performed a back-flip coupled with a 360 over the first big jump, but I landed on the front edge of my board and drove my face into the icy snow like a jackhammer. How I didn't peel my nose right off my face I'll never understand. Still, I placed in the top ten and was happy considering the lack of visibility due to the fog.

The giant slalom event was much more successful. I gave it everything I had, and although I didn't win, I did end up standing on the podium.

Then it came to the mogul day. Head-to-head moguls. Two courses down the same run with two monster-sized jumps at the top and bottom of the course. This was where the National Freestyle Ski Team had been training all summer long, and I'd been riding with them every day.

I made it through all the heats and handily beat my opponents.

The final heat was about to commence, and I found myself vibrating, nervous and excited. I remembered what a friend had once told me: "If you are nervous, then you are on the verge of an opportunity." There I was, about to take advantage of that opportunity. The sun was shining, Mom and Dad were there watching, and Metallica was cranked on the sound system. I was fired up because I knew I was about to pull off a first in snowboarding.

As I hit the first jump, I knew this event was to be mine. I went into the jump with at least fifty percent more speed than I had achieved all day, and as soon as I was going off the lip, I threw my head backwards and started looking for the ground. Yes, folks, I was doing a backflip in the middle of the mogul field. I had been thinking about it all day and knew that it was now or never for that trick. For what felt like a lifetime, I drifted downslope while hanging inverted twelve feet above ground. At this point of the backflip, I could see the spot I was going to land on, and I could hang like that in mid-air until the last possible second when I would tuck my knees and pull my legs back under me. I stomped the landing and continued down at full speed. One more big 360 rotation off the bottom jump, an easy stroll past the finish line, and I knew I had won.

Winning that mogul event and doing so by pulling off a first-ever backflip remains one of my highlights in the sport. It was a big gamble because I was risking it all on landing that one jump. I have thought many times that I chose to risk failure rather than wonder for the rest of my life if I could have landed it.

Snowboard contests slowly transferred into filming and magazine opportunities, and I found I could make a living just by travelling the world with my friends. Between 1988 and 1995, I had at least fifteen different stories printed, as well as over fifty pages of photos. I was also one of the very few snow-boarders in the world to have been on the cover of *Transworld Snowboarding* twice.

Opportunities kept showing up in life, and I kept taking them.

Ken Achenbach told me that we needed to go to Europe to snowboard, and we just had to find a way to get someone else to pay for it for all of us. So, Ken started a tour company called

Ken Ach Adventures. I think I could write an entire book based solely upon the whacky road trips and adventures that we have been on together, and most of the stories would sound totally unbelievable. I was there and I have a hard time believing most of them. With his tour company, we organized trips to Les Arcs, France. Guests flew into Geneva, Switzerland, and we escorted them to Les Arcs and were the mountain tour guides for the week. We ended up going a week early to set everything up and stayed a week after the tours to ride at new resorts and travel around Europe. We would come home with the exact same amount of money we'd left with. It was one of the best plans ever. The first year we went, we kept a diary that a few of us wrote in every day, and we called it, "Europe on someone else's $30 a day." I still have the diary and find myself howling with laughter every time I read it.

As I look back on our European adventures, it constantly amazes me that I am still alive. The places that we went and the insanely steep mountains that we rode, with little to no knowledge of snow or mountain safety, constantly shocks me over how ignorant we were. One day at lunch, we met another French snowboarder who told us he knew a great run down the back of the mountain in Chamonix. Being young and eager, we of course jumped at the idea and off we went into the abyss of the Mer de Glace glacier on the back of the mountain.

I should have known the adventure was going to turn into an epic when we started the run down by rappelling into a 1000-vertical-foot, narrow chute on a crappy nylon rope attached to an old bamboo sign that said, "Danger de mort!" It did not stop us, but we certainly all knew that we were no longer in Kansas. The chute that we descended had huge walls on each side, and the snow we were on was only two metres wide—just wide enough to do a jump turn and not smash into the rocks. By the time we got out of the chute and onto the main path of the glacier, it was starting to get dark. The French snowboarder said that we now had to find the correct exit off our side of the glacier, as we would need to rappel down an icefall, and there was only one place that had a rope in the ice. Other than that, we would be stuck. Eventually, in the waning daylight, we found the rope...more by pure luck than anything else, I might add. This was another yellow nylon rope that was frozen into the ice and hanging down over the ultra-slippery glacier ice. Terrified, we slowly slid, bounced, and slammed our way down the icefall with a snowboard in one hand and trying to hang onto the crappy yellow rope with the other hand. That was something I vowed never to do again.

By some miracle, we made it off the glacier and onto some crazy billy-goat path down the side of the mountain with the twinkling lights of Chamonix in the valley bottom below. Halfway down this path we ran out of snow, and we ended up walking the next three hours back into town. Our friends were down there somewhere in a bar, and cell phones were not a thing yet, so we had no way of telling them that we would arrive about midnight. Upon arrival in town, we headed straight to our favourite bar with snowboard boots still on our feet, soaking wet, and absolutely exhausted. Upon meeting up with our Swedish friends and telling them about another Ken Ach adventure we had been on, they seemed hardly surprised. Somehow, they just knew that was what had happened and there would be a great story in the end.

A normal day in my life as a pro snowboarder.
Photo: Bud Fawcett

Knowing what I know now about snow, glaciers, and mountain safety makes me cringe every time I think about the moronic adventures we went on where somehow we did not die. At that point in life, I was still in the stage of not knowing what I did not know. Luckily, I moved onto the next stage of life called "knowing that I do not know" before life removed me from the gene pool.

Teaching snowboarding and then guiding at Wiegele's was a monumental turning point in my life. At Wiegele's I even found myself teaching some of the most famous big wave surfers in the world. They were coming to me.

Ski guiding ended up being a fulltime job for me after a few years, and snowboarding took a back burner. That was right up until I heard that boardercross racing was going to be in the Olympics. Boardercross is the equivalent of motocross racing on snow. Four riders start at the same time, and the first one across the finish line is the winner. Massive obstacles, rollers, banked turns, and downright scary jumps were the main elements in the design of each boardercross track.

In order to make it to the Olympics, all I had to do was get on the National Boardercross Team and be in the top five. For some reason, every new challenge I take on seems easy to me. I really did, and do, believe that I can do anything in the world. It doesn't always work out, but I certainly believe I can. Some days my eternal optimism is my downfall.

I went in a few local races and placed myself on the podium most days. Then off I went to the Nationals in Montréal, Québec. This was the first time I was racing boardercross against the top in the world, who just happened to be the Canadian National Team. I placed fifth and discovered that maybe my skills needed some serious improvement. Somehow riding powder was not conducive to high-end racing.

For the next two summers, I went to Valle Nevado, Chile for a month to train with a private coach. This was Christian Hrab, who used to be the National Team coach. I thought if anyone knew how to train me, this would be the person.

Christian taught me, through boardercross, a new way to snowboard. He broke down my powder technique and built me back into a racing machine. Now all I had to do was get myself onto the World Cup Tour and onto the National Team. In my head this seemed like a straightforward process. Eternally optimistic.

My greatest asset in the boardercross was my strength and how fast I could react to the gate dropping at the start. In boardercross, there are four racers starting at the same time and there is a five-second window after the start referee says, "Racers ready," when the gate could open. This means that the gate could drop immediately, or up to five seconds later.

Being an older racer had some large advantages, such as that I knew a lot about the human body and how things like our eyesight function. Most racers would stare at the gate and only move once they saw it start to swing towards the ground, whereas I would look down the course and could only see the gate in the bottom of my peripheral vision. That is also where our evolution of survival has taught our eyes to see movement. When other racers stared at the gate, it had to move at least six inches before they were able to perceive movement and react to pull out of the start gate. My eyesight picked up the movement immediately, and I was able to react a tenth of a second before them. As well, I was ten years older than most of my competition and twice as strong. This meant that I could pull out of the start gate faster and harder, and I was always in the lead after the first hundred metres of the race. Once in the lead, it's much easier to win than to try to fight your way back from last place.

Unfortunately, the National Boardercross Organization did not select me as one of the athletes to compete in the 2005 World Cup events. Even though my scores in the NorAm races had qualified me for the events, I was told that at thirty-five I was too old, that there were younger athletes that would have a better chance than me. These were not words that sat well with me. I argued with the board constantly over that issue. On two occasions I had to go to an appeal board in order to obtain my slot for a World Cup start. I realized I needed to get on the tour by a different route.

The winner of the NorAm Championships would get their own spot on the tour. So that's the direction I pointed myself. In 2006, I figured out exactly how many NorAm races I had to enter, where they were, and how I would need to place in them to win the title. It all came down to the final race in Québec. All the National Team would be there, and I was ready. I needed to be in the top three in order to secure my spot on the tour.

The night before the race, it poured rain. One hundred metres in front of the start gate was a massive puddle. Really, it was more like a lake—a foot deep and fifty metres long. The team wax technician and I talked for hours about what to use in order to best conquer this hurdle. In the end, I went with a thick coat of pure silicone on the base of my board, with deep channels gouged down the wax. This would allow my board to glide over the water without it suctioning to the surface. We figured that if I did not slow down in the puddle like the rest of the racers, then I should be in first place every time. Then the aggressive snow would peel the rest of the silicone off, and I would be down to my normal race wax.

This worked flawlessly. Every heat had me in first place, and I moved on to the finals. Now I was up against three other members of the National Team, and they didn't get there by being lucky. These guys were good.

I was first across the puddle but got passed by the world champion on the second corner. He wasn't world champion two years in a row for nothing. At that point I knew I didn't need to win, I just needed to hold my spot in second, and that is exactly what I did. This gave me the NorAm title, and my own spot on the World Cup Tour. I had circumvented the political bullshit of the sport.

A World Cup course is between a minute and thirty seconds to two minutes long. Racers are given two qualifying runs, and the top thirty-two racers move on to the heats. Competitors are separated by mere fractions of a second. If a small technical error was made in the run, then you'd be out of the qualifying. I have never seen another sport with such tight racing times. Some of the races had twenty racers all within one second of each other.

The 2006/2007 winter took me to all the World Cup races around the world. While I excelled at the NorAm races, the World Cup beat down my ego. I went from standing on the podium, to missing the qualifying by one-tenth of a second, which put me in thirty-fifth place. Brute force, determination, and a will to win were being outmatched by youth, agility, and a lack of fear. I was the oldest in the race by ten years or more and was often just referred to as "the Old Man." I was thirty-six years old at the time. Try as I might, I was just not able to perform well enough to knock any existing member of our National Team out of their slot.

I was also starting to feel that I was away from home, from my family, too much, and I began to have second thoughts about this need to make the Olympics.

After returning home from a three-week stretch of competitions, I was having dinner with my family, when my daughter Lydia, who was two, said, "Thank you for dinner everyone. May I be excused from the table?" Wow, this was new to me. Lee said they had been working on manners lately, and this was new in the last week. It was a shocking realization that I was missing out on seeing my kids grow up.

In the end, I came up one spot short of making it into the Olympics. The National Team all made it in, and I was next in line. I had set the bar just one step too high.

The year before the Olympics, I had to decide how much of a life sacrifice I was going to have to make in order to train for boardercross. Two more Chilean-summer months and another winter of being on the road and away. By now I had two daughters and it became clear I was impacting my family more than anything else and was sacrificing raising my children. In the end, the decision to let go of the National Team and Olympic dreams was wise and appreciated.

I've been asked if that was a big disappointment for me, knowing that the Olympics were in Whistler in 2010 and I did not make it. My hometown. But I was extremely content with the effort I'd put forth. Maybe it was better to have set the bar too high and just missed it, rather than having been dissuaded from trying from the start. I was exceptionally proud I had set that as my goal and had tried to achieve yet another dream. I really could not think of a better lesson to teach my children—to set a goal and chase after it no matter the odds that are stacked against you.

My racing career finished, I went back to ski guiding, being an attentive husband, and raising my daughters.

THE TRAMPOLINE INCIDENT

THE YEAR WAS 1990. THE CONTINUATION OF MY EVENTFUL twentieth year...

My friends and I were in Vancouver at the BC Place stadium, offering a trampoline demonstration for snowboarding. We had our boards strapped-on, bouncing on the tramp and doing some cool tricks. There was a crowd of at least 500 people standing around watching. Snowboarding was in its infancy and was still the hot-ticket sport at the time.

I had my burn mask on, but despite that I was still living the dream of a pro-athlete: flanked with fans, friends, music, and beer. It had been six months since the helicopter crash.

I planned to bounce onto the foam pad at the edge of the trampoline and then just hop to the ground. I thought it would look *really cool* to make the exit like that.

Total disaster would be a much better description for what happened.

I tried jumping towards the foam pad, and instead of gently floating forward to the edge, my board slipped out from under me, and I went sailing past the edge of the trampoline and did a swan dive from ten feet up, straight into the concrete. I had both arms stretched out to help break my fall and landed like a ton of bricks. I heard a sickening amount of crunching and snapping as I landed...pretty sure it all came from my body.

I tried to bend my left arm to undo the binding, but the pain and all the little bumps poking up against the skin made me stop. I tried my right arm, and the excruciating pain in the elbow and the inability to move my wrist made me cease that motion as well. That was when I realized I was in a critical state. Both arms were out of commission, and I needed help.

My friends had all come over to see if I was alright. One look in my eyes, and they all knew I certainly was not. They helped me get the board off, stand up, and move away from the trampoline so nobody else could fall on me.

Usually, when a bone breaks, there are at least twenty or thirty minutes before the pain sets in. This gives time to get off to hospital or to get help before the pain becomes unbearable. That was not the case with this crash. By the time I got off to the side and sat down, I was in such intense pain I was barely able to function. There were no positions I could have my arms in without lightning bolts of pain shooting out of the elbows. It really didn't take long to conclude that I'd ruined both elbows and something was also broken in my right wrist. I didn't know enough about anatomy at the time to make a better assessment than that. What I did know was I was fucked.

The ambulance ride was one of the most painful experiences I can remember. I asked the driver if he could only take left turns, as any lean to the right forced the bones to grind against each other.

I sat in the hallway of the emergency room for a long time, waiting for x-rays. They showed that I had broken my right wrist, cracked the radial head of my right elbow, and completely shattered my other radial head. The left elbow was smashed into such small pieces that the surgeon said they would have to operate just to take all the pieces out. I didn't really need the radial head, I was told, as it's a luxury bone! (I'm convinced now, more than ever, that there is no such thing as a luxury bone. They are there for a reason, but that bone is not replaced in elbows. I was told I'd just have to live without it.)

I realized I may have to try to pull off the impossible, yet again.

With both my arms smashed, in slings, and with a cast, I got picked up by my brother Bill, and I stayed at his place.

The first night at Bill's house, he asked me how I was going to brush my teeth. I turned to him and said, "No problem, you brush them." We had a good laugh while he proceeded to gouge my cheeks, poke the brush up my nose, and basically make me bleed.

He then asked about my contact lenses. Again, I gave great directions on how to do that without popping my eyeballs out. It worked, but I had no desire for him to put them back in, so I just wore my glasses for the next couple weeks, as it seemed a whole lot safer.

A bath followed. It felt amazing. Bill even helped to dry me off after. I owe Bill an incalculable debt of gratitude. He became my nurse. But really, this is just what really great brothers do for each other. I'm sure I'd have done the same thing if he had stupidly fallen off a trampoline in front of 500 people and had broken both his arms.

That was when the big question got asked. And I was ready for it. Bill wanted to know how I was going to wipe my ass. I said that I'd been thinking about that and had it covered. I wouldn't need his help. He was so relieved he went and got us beer to celebrate. He delivered mine with a straw.

> *The butt-wiping-with-no-arms-secret:*
> *I used my toes to pick up the bathmat and lay it down on the edge of the bathtub. Yup, you now see exactly where this is going, and I hardly need to explain anymore, but I will. Then, very carefully so as not to bend an elbow, I gently unrolled long sections of toilet paper and smoothly laid them down on top of the bathmat on the tub. I then stepped very gently over and into the tub with one foot, as I really didn't want to slip and fall and break something else while my pants were down. Now, I was set to mimic the dog that wipes its butt on the grass, being exceptionally careful not to soil the bathmat. I never wanted my brother to know exactly how this was being done. As it was, it took me three years to admit to him how I did it.*

The following day, I had to return to the hospital for surgery. The plan was to repair the elbow, if possible, but the surgeon thought it highly unlikely. They thought they would likely only be removing the bone fragments. I was still trying to figure out how the arm would function with that piece of the radial head missing.

The "luxury bone" comment sprang back up, and the doctor assured me that the body does just fine without it. He said it had been done many times before, but he did mention that the downside was that I would lose about fifteen percent of the mobility in the arm. I would not be able to touch my shoulder or straighten my arm again and would also likely lose about twenty percent of my strength. He explained that this is what happens when the scar tissue sets in post-surgery.

I laughed and confidently explained that I knew a fair bit about scar management, and that I would get the full usage of my arm back. He said it wasn't possible, but there might be more surgeries they could do in order to free up the movement in a few years. I explained that I'd done the impossible before and would do it again. And so, out came the "luxury" bone.

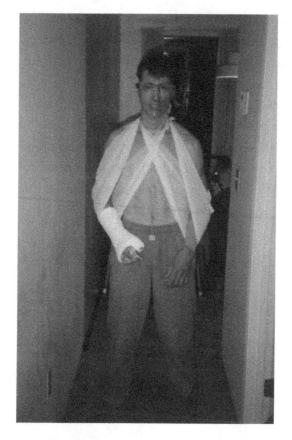

The day after elbow surgery. I weighed 150 pounds.
If there is a low point in my life, this is it.
Photo: Bill Schwartz

Bill had to work, so he called Mom and told her he was putting me on a plane and sending me home. We had, *somehow*, forgotten to call her in the first place. This was the first she was hearing of the accident and surgery. You can imagine her shock. I still hear about this thirty years later.

The day following, Bill dropped me off at the airport with a small bag. I would kick the bag, walk three steps, kick the bag, walk three steps...right up to the ticket counter where I checked in. When I was asked if I had any bags to check, I said no. I got my boarding pass, and off I went down through security and to the boarding gate, kicking my bag the whole way along, both arms in slings, and wearing the mask. What really amazed me was that nobody ever came to ask if they could give me a hand. I guess I could have asked, but that just wasn't in my nature at twenty years old. I still had to do everything myself.

Once I got to the gate and was sitting down, the flight attendant announced over the speaker that if anyone needed pre-boarding assistance, they should approach the gate and get on the plane. I looked around the room and didn't see anyone who fit that description, so I knew we would load soon. Then she made the same announcement. I looked around the room and thought we would soon start loading, as there were no old people or little kids needing help. The woman then walked directly over to me and said very nicely, "Sir, will you please get on the plane so we can all board?" She picked up my bag and I walked onto the plane.

When I was with my parents in Calgary, Halloween came.

I stayed home and gave out candy.

Most kids came to the door, took one look at the scary guy with the mask, plaster, and slung arms, and they backed away. One kid, however, stepped through the door, looked at me and said, "Cool costume, dude! Where's the candy?" I filled his candy bucket to the brim. That kid had just made my year.

The process of healing from all the broken bits took more effort than I ever would have thought.

The easy part was deciding that I would get the mobility back and regain the strength I was told I would never have again. The difficult part was getting the arm to go straight. Within a few months I could touch my shoulder but getting the damn thing to go straight was way harder than I had thought. I would lock my hand between my knees, then wrap a towel around my elbow and force the joint to go as straight as it could. Then I'd pull harder and harder. Some days I was sure I'd just snap the elbow joint in half with how hard I was pulling on that towel, but I was getting closer and closer to straight. I hung from the pull-up bar with one arm and let my body weight try to straighten the elbow. I tried wakeboarding and only hanging on with that arm for the full summer, and I really think this may have been one of the better rehabilitation techniques I used due to the amount of pressure it applied on the joint.

After a year, I came up short by about one degree. There still exists a very slight bend in the elbow and a bit of a kink in the wrist joint. My left arm is now stronger than my dominant right arm. I did every exercise conceivable to regain strength and worked at it hard enough to do one-armed pull ups.

The luxury bone comment from the surgeon came to haunt me fifteen years later. Back pain was starting to creep into my life, and nothing I did was helping to alleviate the pain. In between my shoulder blades it felt like someone was constantly jabbing me with a knife, and it was getting worse every week. I could not sleep, and painkillers had little to no effect. This was serious and I needed to find a solution...and fast. I realized then how easy it would be for someone to get hooked on painkillers. I really would have been happy to try just about anything if it took the constant pain away.

The first doctor I talked to said they would need to fuse two of my vertebrae in order to solve the back-pain problem. I was young, but I knew enough to know that you do not fuse the vertebrae of a thirty-five-year-old who has not had recent major trauma. I knew I had to look outside of the mainstream medical world if I was going to find a cure. Lee's mom suggested I go see a Rolfer in Kamloops, BC. I had no idea what a Rolfer was, but after doing a little research it seemed like something worth trying.

The methodology of Rolfing is the structural reintegration of the body over the skeletal system. The Rolfer will reshape the muscle casing, thus allowing the muscle to go back to its original position, so that the skeleton can realign itself naturally. It is a ten-session procedure, with two weeks of adjustment time between visits. This sounded exactly like what I needed. Body rebalancing.

At the first session, the Rolfer watched me move, walk, sit, stand, twist, and bend and basically observed every piece of movement that my body did for fifteen minutes. With a quizzical look on his face, he asked me what was wrong with my left elbow, as it was slightly bent and was certainly not sitting in a natural state.

After I explained the trampoline crash and the subsequent surgery, he said that I did not have a back problem, but I had an elbow problem. Since the elbow was always bent, it put tension on the bicep, which then pulled on the deltoid, in turn rotating the scapula in my back and causing the back pain. Surgery would have made the entire problem worse.

The Rolfer worked for an hour and a half on my left arm, starting at my fingertips and finishing on my scapula. Some of the work he did felt more like medieval torture, and I really was unsure how that level of pain was going to help. The result, though, was instant relief. I had walked into his office hardly able to breathe due to the pain, and I left one hundred percent pain free and feeling like I was living a new life.

Now, at the age of fifty, my elbow really isn't that big of an issue. I can still do one-armed pull-ups, and I've decided I'm going to keep at it until I'm a hundred. The back pain has never returned, and I've since used the Rolfer to help with many of my injury recoveries.

Once again, I had beaten the impossible.

THE DEATH RACE: QUITTING

TRAINING FOR THE SECOND YEAR OF THE DEATH RACE went differently. I knew I had to avoid the legs seizing, so I grossly increased the amount of effort I put into that area of preparation. I decided to make the training harder than what I thought the race would be.

Three days a week, I woke up at five a.m., threw on the fifty-pound vest (I had yet to get a heavier one), jogged three kilometres over to the base of Whistler Mountain, picked up a thirty-pound rock, ran up to the top of the first chair lift, and dumped the rock in my ever-growing pile. This amounted to a distance of 4000 metres with a twenty-percent grade and a

1500-foot elevation gain. I then ran back down, then home and had breakfast with the family by seven a.m. Rain or shine. Most people couldn't understand why I was doing what I was doing. Trying to explain to people the thrill of pushing your body beyond any limit you ever thought possible was just hard to convey.

The Death Race—and my participation in it, in particular—the second time around, was being filmed by Global Television for a documentary on their show *16x9: The Bigger Picture*. This year, the race "started" on Father's Day. It also happened to be my eldest daughter's birthday and the year-end dance recital for both of my children. The significance of this, as well as the sense of missing out, did not go unnoticed by me.

Betrayal, it just so happened, was the theme in 2012. Trying to anticipate how this would play out in the race was damn-near impossible. Would we be betrayed? Who would betray us? How would I set it up if I was asked? Would moles be planted into the race? How far would the organizers take this? Too many questions, and no real answers.

The gear list contained the same requisite items as the previous year, but this year included a pink swim cap, a life jacket, and one pound of human hair. Again, my pack ended up weighing around fifty pounds. Ten years later, and I still have no idea what the point of the hair was.

The race (or pre-race component) began by having us stand in an icy-cold pond for forty-five minutes. Organizers grouped us into packs of ten. This year, there were 350 competitors. Many I'd seen before, while there were also many fresh, soon-to-be-beaten-down faces amongst the crowd.

Each group was then given an object to carry, which ranged from an eight-foot-diameter tire to a fifteen-foot-long kayak, or the 200-pound, ten-foot-long slosh pipe, half-filled with water. My group was assigned the kayak. We spent the first half hour just holding these items over our heads while the organizing crew shouted and yelled.

These objects then were hauled on a twenty-mile hike through dense forest and steep mountain terrain. Race officials screamed and yelled at everyone, doing their best to demoralize the racers whenever and wherever possible. They did a good job. We had to stop for many one hundred burpee penalties along the way. Burpees no longer bothered me. My pre-race training saw me get to the point where I could do one hundred burpees in four minutes. I would do this multiple times a day.

Twenty miles later, we ended up at a reservoir where we completed a one-mile swim before each having to move twenty bucketloads of gravel to help repave the driveway (the alternative, direct, non-forested way of getting to where we were now). That's when I remembered that this race might just be the best free-labour, make-work project ever...and we were the ones paying for the work to be done. Pure genius. I wish I had thought of it.

A fifteen-mile group run back followed. We thought we were heading back to the main farm...but as it turned out, we weren't. The previous year we had never been more than eight hours from our food cache. Most people only ever brought food and water to last ten hours, at best. I had sustenance for about twenty hours, but it had been well over twenty-four hours since our departure from the farm. Most everyone was out of food and wouldn't drink the water out of the creeks as we were told (all lies!) that it was full of giardia...the infamous and dreaded "beaver fever." I drank out of every stream that we came across, and I foraged trail-side clover by the ton. If the sheep like the stuff, why not me? Better than starving. I was not going to "betray" my caloric needs. At many points I was seen to pick up handfuls of wet moss, hold it over my face, and squeeze the water into my mouth. I thought that this was great thinking, but most others just looked at me like I was a lunatic.

We were brought to a halt for two hours to write a 300-question test. I was sure the idea was to make us sit, wish we had food, and stiffen up like a pretzel in the sun. I did part of the test and concluded that it had nothing to do with the race. I was confident that there was a zero percent chance they could mark all 300 of the tests, so I went looking for food.

They told us that if our support crew gave us food, we would be disqualified, which I interpreted as meaning I could beg, borrow, or steal food from anyone else or from anyone else's support crews. The family of a fellow racer was sitting at a park bench eating a pizza, and I went over and very politely told them I was a Death Racer and was taking their pizza. I brought it back to my small crew and we feasted like this was our last meal. I still remember the look of total disbelief on the faces of the family as they watched us eat their stolen pizza like a pack of starved jackals. Sorry.

Searching all over a densely forested hillside for a marker with your team's number on it became the next activity. We didn't get to pick who our team of four was. I wound up with—what felt like in that moment—the three most useless individuals on the planet. In the search for our flag, I ran ten kilometres all over the hill. They all simply gave up after five minutes. The sense, or a sense of, betrayal was beginning to set in.

Chopping a giant log into five-foot lengths, then splitting it into pieces of firewood was the next stage. We then had to carry it back over the mountain to get to the farm, and that was when the race would officially start. Here I got lucky, as it took me so long to find my flag on the hillside that they only had medium-sized logs left to chop. My buddies, who'd gotten there an hour before me, had absolute monster slabs of wood to deal with. Score another for the unfair race working in my favour. I bucked up my piece of log with my hand saw, then went full-savage with the axe to split it into manageable pieces to load onto my pack. Directions pertaining to what route I would need to follow to get back to the farm were given to me, and off I ran. Some thirty hours after we began, we were back at our food.

The same as last year, I had a one-pound hamburger with a quarter pound of butter and welded it together with almond butter. I was going to burn off the 3000 calories over the next three hours.

Log rolling came next. No, we didn't roll logs around. Instead, we each had to roll like a log around a one-kilometre loop, ten times in 30°C heat. There also just happened to be a festering, boiling bucket of cow entrails that we had to stir half the way around. At the end of each lap there was a skill-testing question. If you got the answer wrong, your lap was voided. Did you know that a four-ring archery target has five zones? I didn't.

At that point in the race, I was travelling with Ken Lubin and PJ Rakowski. I had met them the previous year, and both were absolute beasts when it came to the event. PJ was a high school gym teacher who could step off the couch and run a four-hour marathon like it was nothing. Ken ran "Executive Athletes" out of Boston. He had the best attitude in the world when it came to suffering, misery, and adventure racing. As we travelled together for the latter half of the race, we became known as the "Rat Pack," The event had become fun.

When Ken, PJ, and I first arrived at the log rolling, they told us we had to roll fifteen laps of the field. Upon examining the field, we determined that this was probably not possible. I borrowed the radio from one of the volunteers and contacted Joe Desena, who was the chief of the race. I told him that there was no way the Rat Pack was rolling fifteen laps of the field, and that he had to come up with a better plan. We said three would be suitable.

There was a very long pause before Joe and I finally bartered the rolling down to six laps. I had no idea if six laps was the original plan and they were just messing with us, or if I had succeeded in my negotiations. I doubt I'll ever know, but at least I tried.

Rolling like a log for a kilometre sounds darned impossible without puking. So, I suggested that we roll four times in one direction, then flip head to foot and roll four times the other way. This way we hopefully would end up not nearly as nauseated. That technique ended up as pure genius, as none of us puked on the first two laps. On the fourth lap, though, I puked. I had gotten a whiff of the percolating hot cow guts. Holy cow! Up until then I had been holding my breath when I stirred it, and this one time, I forgot. I felt quite lucky to eventually be able to roll away from the violent, body-puking spasms that incapacitated me for five minutes.

Following the log rolling event, we were ordered to pick up a sixty pound sack of concrete, and told to deliver it to the top of the mountain. One of the organizers wanted to build a rock cabin at the top of the hill, and this was certainly the cheapest way to transport all the concrete up there. The route up was directly in the middle of a cascading creek bed, going up a forty-five-degree hillside. Nobody had said any of this was going to be easy.

I discovered that in the Death Race, I sometimes needed to entertain myself, and watching other people and their reactions to the race was the best entertainment going. On the hike back to the top of the mountain with a sixty-pound sack of concrete over my shoulder, I ran into an exhausted-looking guy who was coming downhill with his pile of firewood. He asked me if the concrete bag was his next task, and I had to inform him of all the fun tasks he was going to do before getting to that point. I said that he was at least six to eight hours away from getting to the concrete part. The guy responded by dropping his firewood on the ground and mumbling, "The fuck I am." He quit and headed home. For that guy, knowing too much was his downfall.

Concrete hauled, I had to then carry another fifty-pound log up a hill. Reaching the top, I was to read the instructions on how to fold an origami swan. I *still* have no idea what the ever-difficult, inside-out reverse fold is. I do, however, remember that together, we tried to figure it out for a very *looooong* time before we settled on our crap version: a somewhat-lacking paper bird. We moved onto the next checkpoint and somehow our birds passed inspection.

It was getting dark and we had been on the go for over sixty-three hours. Ken, PJ, and I were, at this point, about five hours in front of the next person. We had covered close to eighty miles of mosquito-infested swamps, lakes, creeks, and rivers, lugging forests of downed trees and rocks, which had come into being eons ago. We had done thousands (yes, thousands) of burpees and now it was time to finish it. Or at least we hoped...

As we arrived back at the farm, we realized this was *not* the end. I don't think enough people had quit yet to make organizers happy. We were ordered to turn around, get a bucket of river gravel, and deliver it to the top where the concrete was dropped off. I do believe the response from all three of us in unison was: "Fuck off!" We went and sat down and started drinking beer.

We quit.

I quit.

Quitting seemed like the smartest thing we had ever done. We were in the lead by six hours now, and we were just sick of going up and down the same freaking mountain and doing all somebody else's free construction work. In our minds, we had shown that race who we were. Our quitting-in-protest felt, in this moment, like winning the race. We'd made a stand, and we would be remembered for that. Oh, we were remembered all right. Remembered as quitters.

I called my daughters, and my seven-year-old, Lydia, asked me why I had quit. I told her I hadn't quit, that I had stopped due to boredom. She told me I was quitting and asked again why I quit. She continued that "our family was not a bunch of quitters." In that moment, I realized that I had inadvertently betrayed my daughter, my family, and ultimately myself.

The Death Race had won; it had broken me.

I'd let frustration beat me.

The race had succeeded in doing what it was supposed to do. It had defeated me. Or at least it had pissed me off to a point where I made a poor decision at a time when I was highly emotional. I was exasperated from being awake for seventy hours, hiking eighty miles while carrying one hundred pounds on my back, and doing the world's most ridiculous tasks. I had done this to myself. I had entered a race that brings out the best in us, the worst in us, and the most out of us, all at the same time. Perhaps, in some sense—in hindsight—I had won. The second time around, my win had been the opportunity to taste defeat, to appreciate a very tangible—and uncomfortable—sense of personal betrayal.

I knew immediately what I had to do.

I signed up for next year.

I am not a quitter.

I am someone who can do *anything* and keep on smiling. I have survived a helicopter crash, broken arms, a smashed nose, and I now needed to prove to my daughter that you can do anything when you set your mind to it.

Success next year was my only option.

Either that or I really would die trying.

THE BROKEN LEG

EVERY YEAR, MOM CELEBRATES HER BIRTHDAY BY BRINGing her children's families together at Sunshine Village for a weekend of skiing. My brother and his kids come, along with my sister and her husband, and me and my wife and daughters. We ski, eat, drink, and just generally have the best weekend of skiing of our year.

In 2019, Lee and I moved ourselves and our two girls to Québec for two months. We wanted to offer our daughters the opportunity to be fully immersed in French culture. Having already been in the French immersion program in Whistler, they were enrolled in French school in Sherbrooke. We felt this experience would allow them to become fully fluent, as well as being a great experience for Lee and me, both Anglophones.

In the middle of our Quebec stay, we came back to the Sunshine Lodge for my mom's birthday. Late afternoon on our second day, we were all skiing together and stopped mid-mountain, just above a very steep, icy slope. The light was flat. We could see the lodge in the distance, and I knew that everyone, including myself, was near the end of their day.

We pushed off down the hill and I made two sloppy turns, crossed my left ski over my right, and fell forward on my face. It was at slow speed, no big deal, not dramatic, and it really looked like a non-event. As a result, everyone giggled at my falling over and popping up with a face-full of snow.

It was funny right up to the point where I told them I had just broken my leg. The laughing stopped.

Here we were, on the iciest run of the mountain and a long way from the lodge. Someone asked if I was sure it was broken.

I had heard the snap and the pain was intense. There was no doubt.

Lee suggested we call the Ski-Patrol for a toboggan rescue. As a mountain guide, I frequently deal with people who have sustained injuries, and I understand a lot about first aid and rescue. I did not want patrollers taking me down the forty-degree ice pitch on a sled. I didn't doubt that they were highly skilled, but I trusted my own abilities far more than I was willing to trust theirs.

I got up, put my ski back on, and told everyone I'd meet them at the bottom, at the patrol shack. The pain was astounding, but I knew that I had about twenty minutes before the real pain, if any, was going to show up. In my head, I was processing how long it was going to take to get to the first-aid hut, down the gondola, then into the town of Banff to get the x-ray and result, have dinner, and make it back up onto the hill before the end of the night.

One-legged skiing really isn't that hard. Add ice, a steep slope, and the feel of broken bones grating together every time the ski hits a bump, and *then* it becomes not quite as easy as it sounds. Okay, I'll admit, it doesn't sound easy when worded like that.

I made it all the way down to the patrol shack with only a few deep-breathing-pain-management stops enroute. Otherwise, it was uneventful.

After I checked in at the Banff hospital, the orthopedic doctor came to see me. His first comment was, "Oh, you're Don Schwartz. Heard lots about you." I had an established record of hospital visits. The Banff hospital was also where I'd had my ACL repaired and a chunk of bone pulled out of my ankle twenty years before.

The x-ray showed a broken fibula—just slightly above the ankle—called a Weber fracture. The doctor made a couple of quick phone calls with a few other orthopedic surgeons, and they decided that a cast was not needed. It was also determined that surgery wouldn't be required, and it was best to put me in a plastic boot and send me home. With a ridiculously high pain tolerance, I opted not to take any pain medications.

I was to be non-weight-bearing for the next six weeks. This was not the news I wanted to hear but had somehow suspected I would. I said that was not possible, as I was running a ten-kilometre race in Whistler in six weeks. I needed a second opinion.

The second opinion was that I was nuts and should go home and keep off the leg for six weeks. Evidently, and understandably, this new doctor knew nothing of my history or the healing tools that I had at my disposal. Personally, I knew I'd be up and running in six weeks, I just needed to convince the rest of the world of it too. I guessed the easiest way was just going to be to show them, and I immediately started a program of supplements and meditative visualization.

We had one day left at the lodge before returning to Québec. Upon return, I went and saw an orthopedic surgeon, who looked at my new x-ray and asked how many weeks ago I had broken my leg. I told him it had been five days. He double-checked the x-ray and informed me that wasn't possible, because the bone showed lots of new growth. I told him what I'd been doing for the past five days, and why the bone was healed as well as it was, listing what supplements I had been taking and the amount of visualization I had been doing. He just looked at me with a blank stare.

Getting to the hospital to see this surgeon had been monumentally challenging. We had picked Sherbrooke, Quebec, to live in because it was very French, and it would be a very challenging town to live in if you did not speak French. I mostly discovered this when going to the emergency room at the hospital, when the first person who spoke English was the surgeon I talked with one hour later. To get past the registration nurse and the triage nurse, I'd discovered the full power of Google Translate. That app really is the new Star Trek communication device. With Google Translate, my sloppy French, and lots of waving my arms, I was able to navigate the system and get to see the surgeon. I'm most proud of this achievement in my healing.

I never travel without my Bemer pad. The Bemer is a PEMF (pulsed electromagnetic field) device that stimulates the capillary response in the body. With this injury, I had been sleeping on it and using it at least eight hours a day to help with blood circulation and swelling reduction. Using it encourages blood to move more like a garden hose and less like a slinky. With increased blood flow, there is better oxygenation of the cells and better perfusion as well as a decrease in swelling. And since I wasn't running around on my leg, I had plenty of time to meditate and visualize the bones healing back together one cell at a time. I'd done it with my nose and my ear, so this was just another chance to use the same skills on my leg.

I pictured the same little green men employed in my burn recovery, now carrying new bone cells, calcium, magnesium, and little balls of green energy from the core of my body down to the broken bone and rebuilding it one cell at a time. I did this for at least five hours a day, along with using the Bemer pad, ice/heat therapy, and taking every bone-building supplement I could find. I may not have known exactly what helped the most, but I didn't have time to try things one at a time. I only had five weeks left before I was to be out running.

With enough positive belief and a burning desire to heal, I knew I could heal my leg in record time. I just needed to add a few more healing methods to the mix.

I went to see an acupuncturist in Sherbrooke. After the first treatment, the swelling in my leg dropped in half. After the second treatment, I felt like I was ready to run. I also went to the CrossFit gym five days a week. I focussed on the rowing machine, push-ups, pull-ups, and just about everything else that could be done while balancing on one leg or sitting down. After a month, my shoulders and upper body were stronger than they had ever been, and I had abs of steel.

Back in Whistler with one week to go before race time, I was now fast walking on my leg. There was no pain, and the most recent x-ray showed that the bone was almost fully healed. The clinic doctor informed me the x-ray looked great for a three-month-old break. I corrected her, saying it had only been five weeks, and he thought I was joking. I had to show her the date on the original x-ray to get her to believe it.

Race day arrived. I must admit that I downscaled my ambitions a bit and chose to do the five-kilometre run, not the ten. It's great to be tough, to heal fast, and to make a fabulous comeback, but there is also a point where you just need to be smart. I was making the smart choice. My pace wasn't fast, and I wasn't going to beat any records, but I also didn't come in last.

I'm not saying that every person should ignore the advice of their doctor. Not at all. What I am saying is that when you are motivated, when you want something badly enough, when you have the burning desire to achieve it, the impossible does not enter the picture. I do not think I am an anomaly in this world, I'm just an example of what a person can do when they firmly believe something can be done.

If you believe it strongly enough, then anything is possible.

OWNING A HELI-SKIING COMPANY

I HAD ALWAYS WONDERED IF BEING AN OWNER OF A SNOW-cat-accessed ski business was for me, so the offer to become a partner in Powder Mountain Catskiing was not to be turned down. I had heard many great things about the place, and several of my friends were working for them.

I had just come from Mike Wiegele Heli-Skiing, which was in the upper echelon of the helicopter ski operators in the world. On any given day we were dealing with twelve helicopters and one hundred and twenty guests. The logistics of managing that many moving parts required a high level of refined finesse. I was also aware that there was a growing market for such, witnessing first-hand how much people were willing to pay for an epic back-country experience. I had a dream of what I could achieve if I took on the Powder Mountain endeavor, and I had the burning desire to see it come to fruition.

If I wanted to succeed, then I would need to get Powder Mountain up to a much higher standard than where it was currently operating. This was going to be a monumental task for the beleaguered company. Significant equipment upgrades and operational system refinement were both required, as well as cash flow. I was up to the challenge, but I just did not have a true appreciation of how much effort it was going to take. I would find out soon enough.

Powder Mountain is eighteen kilometres south of Whistler, off the Sea to Sky Highway. It was first established in 1996 and my involvement began in 2003. Newly married, Lee and I had moved to Whistler and were expecting our first child.

I had Wiegele as an example. When he first began building, everyone told him he was crazy, that it wouldn't work. But he had a dream, and nobody was going to stop him from achieving it. His outlook, akin to my own, was inspiring. This was how I was styling myself moving forward.

I knew scant little about how to run the business end of a business. I just knew what the end product had to be, and what we had to be doing to provide that product. Deep down, I knew that if we could get the service up to the standard I wanted, then the rest of the business would fall into place. How to get there was the challenge.

By the end of the first year of operations, we had made some significant changes within the company and were now providing a service near what I was hoping for. The guides were a little frustrated with me at the start because of how many drastic changes were suddenly implemented. However, by the middle of the season they all agreed that things ran much more smoothly now. This was further reinforced by the larger tip amounts that were being collected. All of this was positive.

By the end of the first season, I found myself writing a very large cheque to keep the company afloat. This is where my lack of business knowledge had come to bite me on the ass. I was risking financial ruin. How I was going to get past it, I really had no idea, yet. I just knew that I wanted to succeed. I was not going to accept failure on this one.

The company had a very unusual, rather complex, arrangement of owners. There was a fifty/fifty split for one share between me and two great friends from the snowboarding world, while other fractions were held by other partners. Everyone wasn't on the same page. There was no easy way to get major decisions made. There were too many people who thought they were all in charge and were going in different directions. Visions didn't align. We didn't have a direction or focus. This mess had to change.

My half of the company discovered a fabulous general manager. Every company needs a "no" person, that somebody who can be the company asshole when need be. The one to be the hard-liner that the business requires to succeed. We had that person, and he worked out incredibly well. The other side of the ownership was a little less enamoured with him, as their scams and fraud were being found out and shut down. Stringent changes were made.

As events unfolded over the next year, I was able to buy out one partner, and I now had control over the voting rights in the company. This helped smooth out the day-to-day operations and the pocketbook.

There were further shifts in partners and holdings. The old guard slipped away, and new breath was inserted into the company's resurgence. A new partner arrived with financial backing and a whole lot more business knowledge than I had. It now looked like I was not going to have to sell my house in order to keep the company alive at the end of the year. This is no joke, as this was something I'd been considering.

There really is not a way to get past years of the stress of potential financial ruin without it affecting your daily health. I feel this too contributed, in part, to the PTSD that would surface in years to come.

Powder Mountain now had new snowcats, great staff, and an incredible general manager. All we needed now was snow. If the skies would cooperate, we could make the rest of the business work. For the next three years, that was all it did...snow. We had three of the biggest snow years in Whistler's history. Timing was everything...and the heavens were conspiring in our favour.

What's more, 2010 was the year of the Olympics in Whistler. We needed to add more to the company to step up our game and increase business, so we added helicopter skiing.

The local helicopter company had the land tenure rights to a massive area of skiable terrain to the south of Whistler, which Powder Mountain was right in the middle of. This was a match made in heaven. We built two landing pads at the base of our lodge, and now we were in the heli-ski business too. I was in my element. Thirteen years as a lead guide at Wiegele's had taught me how to make that aspect function seamlessly *and* turn a profit.

The profit line of the business turned around, and I no longer feared financial ruin. Not all years were like that, though. After some seasons, I wrote larger cheques than I made in salary during the winter. However, these managed to balance out. A bad year would be followed by a booming, flush season, it always seemed.

The company had phenomenal staff. They became a tight group who all understood the intent of the operation: to get all the guests from the village to the snowcat and up on the hill skiing, offering them a comparable-to-none experience throughout. Whatever it took to get that accomplished was everyone's job. Everybody pitched in. Nobody in the company was above toilet cleaning.

Taking my family heli-skiing is one of the perks of ownership.
Photo: Richard Gray

Not all dreams last a lifetime, though, as I soon realized.

My children began calling me "the grizzly bear," the staff were wondering why I was so grumpy, and my wife was questioning why I was sleeping so poorly. It was 2018. I was no longer a nice, polite person, nor was I happy. I was not enjoying my days going out helicopter skiing in the blue skies and sunshine.

If heli-skiing is not making you happy, then there must be a problem.

Ten years of going to bed at midnight and waking up at four-thirty a.m. matched with the continual stress of potential financial ruin makes one a grumpy beast. After a while, I stopped liking myself. This was the place I always vowed that I would never let myself get to. Yet here I was.

In the middle of that challenging winter, I had three people approach me with inquiries as to how they could buy into the cat-skiing business. I turned them all down, but then soon came to realize that this might be what I was looking for. The more I started thinking about it, the more I realized this was the opportunity knocking again, and I'd best at least look in the door.

I was very proud of the accomplishments that I'd been part of and thought that maybe now was the time to find the next chapter of my life. I had taken a near-defunct operation and in six years helped turn it around. Many of my friends were employed there, and I really did love skiing. I just did not like who I was becoming.

I woke up the next day, phoned my business partner, and asked if he was interested in taking over the whole company. I would stay on as the guiding operations manager, but just would no longer be the owner. We had a deal. And I had suddenly shed off all my stress.

It took a year to close the deal, but in that time, I was revitalized back into the happy and positive, forward-looking guy that I had been before. My daughters dropped the nickname, my health improved, quality sleep returned, and my relationship with my wife was blossoming again. I also found a whole new love for skiing that I didn't know had gone missing.

I still work at Powder Mountain. My job is guiding operations manager. I go out in the mountains every day, ski powder, get paid, and am living in Whistler with my family. I have no idea how to make life any better than it currently is.

ON BECOMING A PARENT

NOT EVERYTHING IN LIFE GOES THE WAY THE STORYBOOK says it should. Having a child should be the most amazing experience of one's life and be filled with joy and comfort. It should not be filled with unknowns, anxiety, and concern.

Lee and I had the perfect plan on how to prepare for, conceive, nurture, and birth our first child. We started one year in advance by cutting out alcohol and caffeine and started eating only organic foods in order to have our bodies in pristine condition for conception.

We were absolutely convinced we would conceive this child in the first month of Lee's cycle, and nine months later this baby would be born at the exact time of the year we had planned upon, which was January or February. We already had a parenting plan set out as to how we would raise our child for its first year. We were the perfect parents-to-be, with the perfect plan.

In the ski-guiding world, there is an expression: "Make a plan so that we know what we are *not* doing." A plan is a great starting point, but in the end, you often find yourself following something that looks nothing like the original idea. This is what happened to Lee and me.

We did not conceive in the first month. Neither had we succeeded after seven months. I went in for fertility testing to see if my sperm were the issue. They were fine. We tried as many things as there were ideas for successful conception. None seemed to be working. In the end, we conceived on the night where Lee had said that there was no point tonight, as we had missed the window for the month. Funny how the world works.

The pregnancy progressed normally for a few months, then Lee went in for a regular fetal ultrasound to see how things were developing. We were expecting great news. Instead, we received concern, questions, and more specialists than could have been anticipated.

Lee had gone in for the ultrasound with her mom while I was working. Several ultrasound technicians cycled through. They told Lee the baby was very active, and they could not get the pictures they wanted. The technicians reassured Lee and her mom, but Lee was concerned. We went to see her doctor for the follow-up appointment.

We were told to wait for a follow-up ultrasound in four to six weeks. Lee was devastated, like being kicked in the gut. We did not tell anyone. We really had nothing to say.

We waited until our physician friend Harold arrived and we told Harold. He was upset and wanted to help us find out about our unborn baby. He booked an ultrasound for us in Vernon. The ultrasound went well, but poor Harold had to tell us the options.

1. Baby was fine.

2. Baby had heart problems

3. Lee was carrying a non-viable fetus.

I can't possibly imagine what Harold went through with having to tell his friends this kind of news about their baby.

We were referred to the Children's Hospital in Vancouver to get a better assessment.

Two weeks later, we were sitting in a conference room in the hospital with counsellors, doctors, nurses, specialists, and two pediatric heart surgeons. There we were told that our child had tricuspid stenosis. This means that the intake valve on the right side of the heart does not work properly, limiting the growth of the right side of the heart. They said that when the child was born, they would be able to do a couple of different surgeries to redirect the blood flow around the right side of the heart, straight to the lungs. It would take time, but the problem was repairable.

We broke down in tears. We were not crying out of sorrow. These were tears of joy. Our baby would live!

We had come to the hospital that day having steeled ourselves in preparation for hearing that we had a non-viable fetus. Upon hearing that our child could still be born and would just need surgery, we became the most relieved parents on the planet. The tears flowed freely.

Fast forward to the day that our daughter was to be born. The doctors told us we had to have the baby at the Children's Hospital, as that was where the surgical team would be on standby to intervene if necessary. Nobody knew how the baby would do after birth. Surgery might be needed that day or maybe not for a year. We moved to Vancouver a month prior to delivery.

My brother Bill lived two blocks from the hospital and was gracious enough to allow us to move into his house for as long as we needed. Of any family in the world that understood the needs of new parents with a baby in the hospital, it was his. Their son had been born eleven weeks premature and spent that whole eleven weeks in neonatal intensive care. Our families have been through much.

At this point, we did not know the sex of our child, as we felt this was the greatest surprise in life. After eight hours of labour, a beautiful baby girl arrived, kicking and screaming. She was a little bit blue due to her heart not providing full oxygenation, but there she was...alive, and ours.

Lydia ended up having multiple rounds of open-heart surgery to re-route the blood flow in her body. All the returning blood flow was now going straight to the lungs, bypassing the right side of her heart. She functions with only the left side of her heart pumping blood and venous flow to her lungs.

Our daughter was expected to be small, weak, and severely challenged by her lowered heart function. She is my child, though, and did inherit my stubbornness to not always accept the diagnosis given.

When Lydia was born, we were told only about the limitations presented for her. If she played soccer, she could be a goalie. She would have difficulties with anything athletic. Our decision was that we would do everything humanly possible to give her the best chance she could have. All our food would be organic. All our efforts would be towards perfect health and nutrition. We would never cease in our effort to find ways for her to succeed. It was decided that if she did not thrive in her life, it would only be due to her heart and certainly not because we were told that was the way it was supposed to be.

Not once in Lydia's life did we ever tell her she would be limited by her body or that she would be weaker or slower than anyone else. Setting limitations upon someone before they have a chance to try did not seem fair.

At sixteen years old, Lydia is 5'8" tall, rides mountain bikes, water-skis, climbs mountains, is an exceptional skier, and can run a five-kilometre race in thirty minutes. She is the exact opposite of weak, frail, and challenged and the total anomaly amongst the children that have her heart condition. She truly is one of a kind.

Every day I take strength and motivation from Lydia as I see her blossoming into a young adult and tackling every challenge that life presents. She has become my new hero.

Our second child, Stella, arrived twenty months after our first. We were shocked at how fast Stella was conceived.

It was International Burn Survivors Day. April 12. I had the honour of delivering the end-of-conference "Thank You" speech to Kim Phuc. Phuc was the little girl on the infamous cover of *Time* magazine in 1972, photographed while running down the street in Vietnam after having been severely burned by napalm. The iconic shot is unforgettable. If you have ever seen the photo, you would remember it.

Lee was attending the conference with me. We were expecting her to go into labour any day, but we thought we had plenty of time to be at the conference, enjoy the speech, and have at least an extra day or so before active labour would start. Were we wrong!

Just as the speeches started, Lee grabbed my arm, as she was rocked by a major contraction. She told me I should stay and give my speech and then meet her at the hospital.

Lee went to the front of the hotel, where a doorman realized she was going into labour, and he jumped into the middle of the street to flag down a taxi. I stayed at the conference and mulled over my speech one more time to make sure I was ready.

After five minutes of sitting, I realized that I was most certainly required elsewhere! My wife would need me, and I was not going to miss the birth of my child. I mentioned to the organizer that I had to go as Lee was in labour. I handed her my speech and was out the door.

I arrived in the nick of time at the hospital, and I was with Lee as she delivered our second beautiful little girl. My timing was perfect.

The things that kids do can be the most inspiring events in a person's life. At eighteen months old, Stella did very little talking, as her sister translated everything for her. Then, Stella walked in from the hot tub, and stated, "Mommy, I had fun in hot tub!" She went from needing no words at all to speaking in full sentences in one day. I'm still in awe of how kids can do this, as it most certainly seems impossible.

It was when Stella was two that I saw how kids can do anything if only they are given a chance. My wife and I had been teaching Stella to water-ski by starting her on the shore and pulling her by hand up to the back of the boat, where she would stop on the swim platform. We did this about a hundred times. Then on attempt one hundred and one, we started to drive away while she was only halfway to the boat, and just like that Stella was water-skiing on the long rope. She proceeded to do a full lap of the lake, while waving at all the people on shore like royalty in a parade. My eyes still tear up when I think about that day.

Stella, now fourteen, is equally as active and gregarious as her older sister, while very much being her own person. She dreams of becoming a race car driver, and Lydia, a vet. The two of them collaborate on a successful, summer-market stall venture, selling organic, homemade peanut butter. They are the Peanut Butter Queens. The two of them never cease to amaze me, inspiring me day-in, day-out.

Parenting is certainly not without its tougher moments, and I have been through more of those tough moments that anyone should ever have to. My whole family has tested every aspect of my first aid skills, from broken collar bones to full blockage choking situations, to a traumatic brain injury.

I started the problems by taking both kids on a horseback ride, while I was leading the horse. What I didn't know about horses was that when they are separated from their herd, they act like a freak on acid. As I rounded the barn, the horse bucked, and both kids went flying like they were shot out of a cannon. There are few things in life that can scare a parent more than seeing both their kids sailing through the air to then land flat on their faces in the dirt. Epic parenting fail on my part.

Stella was unhurt, but Lydia ended up with a major concussion and a broken collar bone. On the drive to the hospital, Lydia kept asking why she was sitting in Stella's car seat. She asked that ten times in the ten-minute drive to the hospital.

The next major event was when Lydia fell while barefoot water-skiing and ended up with a major brain bleed. She was on aspirin as a blood thinner for her heart, and this led to the brain bleed becoming more and more severe. We loaded into the minivan, and a friend who is a nurse was in the backseat with Lydia while I drove and Lee was on the phone with the 911 operator.

Lee said the 911 operator told us to pull over and wait for the ambulance. My response was to yell, "Fuck that" at the phone, and I said that we could meet the ambulance half-way. It was a thirty-minute drive to the nearest hospital at that time, and I was not sitting around waiting for the ambulance.

Meanwhile, in the backseat, my friend was giving out vital signs to pass onto the ambulance that we were going to meet, and he said, "I have a pulse!" Which to me meant that at one point, there was no pulse. Apparently, the look on our faces was so intense that he followed it up with, "I have a pulse rate! There has been a pulse all along." Nothing in a parent's life can prepare you for a situation like that.

I probably should not have been driving the van in that terrorized condition, but it certainly did not make me slow down from the 180 kilometres an hour that I was driving. By the time we met the ambulance, the brakes were smoking, and the tires had been nearly shredded off the rims. Who knew that the minivan was a highspeed rally mobile?

Lydia was flown to Children's Hospital in Vancouver where she stayed in the ICU for two days and then spent another eight days in the trauma ward. The first twenty-four hours scared Lee and me into cardiac arrest, as Lydia went into a brief coma and the surgeons were preparing to operate. Upon them inserting an IV into Lydia's arm, she woke up screaming and complaining about the needle poke. Surgery was cancelled, and parental relief was beyond belief.

In order to reduce the swelling in Lydia's head, we resorted to every tool in our toolbox. We had the acupuncturist come into the hospital to help. The Bemer pad was used daily and rapidly the swelling reduced. The medical experts were honest enough to say they didn't know how to assist in the swelling removal in the head, but I certainly knew ways that we could try. Not trying every possible avenue would be like quitting, and I knew not to do that again.

The LENS Neurofeedback system was also used with great results to help in the concussion recovery. Within two months of the horrific traumatic brain injury, Lydia was back running five kilometres, and our family went on a cruise to Alaska. (The upcoming chapter on flying and PTSD will explain everything about the LENS system.)

The third major parenting test was provided by Stella. The family was driving through Kamloops, BC, when Stella said she was a bit itchy. Then she became extremely itchy. Then she needed to stop on the side of the road for a bathroom break. We could see large welts forming on her skin, and then she mumbled out that she was having a hard time breathing.

I knew immediately what this was from all my first aid work. Stella was going into anaphylactic shock. Reacting to what, I had no idea. I only knew that we had to get to the hospital and get there fast. It looked like it was time to see how fast the minivan could go again.

Once again, Lee was on the phone with the 911 operator, and I was driving like I stole it. This time when we were told to pull over and wait for the ambulance, Lee was able to tell them to get the ER team ready as we would be at the front door of the hospital within minutes, and Stella needed an EpiPen immediately.

I really would suggest that this is not the best option for most people. When events like this are occurring, we as parents are certainly not functioning at our best, and it took a monumental amount of effort to concentrate on high-speed driving and not being distracted by my rapidly fading daughter. Had I not been through such daunting situations with my family before, there is no way I would have been able to pull this off. Success was also because my wife is so powerfully strong and could deal with Stella and the 911 operator at the same time without becoming hysterical. Separating emotions from the situation may be one of the hardest parenting tasks ever. I really hope nobody ever needs do what we did.

I pulled into the front of the Kamloops hospital with smoke blowing off the tires, while Lee jumped out with Stella and handed her to the waiting ER team. They took one look at Stella and jabbed her with the EpiPen. Within minutes her breathing returned to normal, and her symptoms started to subside. Four hours later, we left the hospital to stay at a local hotel for the night. There was no way we were leaving town when we still had no idea what she had reacted to.

In the following years, we tried every resource we could find to track down the offending item that caused the anaphylactic shock, with no luck. To this day, we still do not know. Stella carries an EpiPen, and we are not sure what she is allergic to. This is challenging to tell new instructors when she goes to an activity, as the conversation goes like this:

"Stella has an EpiPen."

"What is she allergic to?"

"We do not know. But she has her pen."

I feel so sorry for the people that coach my kids and run into things like this.

Life calmed significantly after these episodes, and maybe the world consciousness decided that I had been tested enough, and it was time to leave my family alone.

Parenting certainly turned out far different than I ever would have suspected. Luckily all the good events outweigh the hard times. Some events in life I think are just there to remind me of vital life clues, and sometimes I only became aware of them much later.

The Burn Fund in Vancouver sent beautiful flowers the week after Stella's birth and informed me that my thank you speech to Kim Phuc was one of the more emotionally moving closing speeches they had ever heard. So emotionally powerful that it brought the room to tears. I recall the last line of my speech: "No matter how hard you think you have it, someone else has been through worse and they are still here."

BAREFOOT WATER-SKIING

BAREFOOT WATER-SKIING FIRST CAME ABOUT IN 1947 AS
A.G. Hancook took to the water in Winter Haven, FL. Dick
Pope Jr, who was a world-famous water-skier, was next up to
tackle the sport. This was all happening in Cypress Gardens, FL,
which is the home of all the sports and water-ski shows.

The sport started by the skier stepping off a water ski onto
their feet. It gradually progressed into doing beach starts and
then what is called a deep-water start. Slowly, different tricks
were added as the skiers became more proficient and more
people joined the sport.

Barefoot water-skiing requires ridiculously high speeds,
nerves of steel, a solid mental belief that you won't die, and an
acceptance that death might be a possibility. It is an *extreme* sport.

In 1996, I had just purchased a cabin in the Cariboo region
of BC. Twenty kilometres away, one of the ski guides I worked
with said I should come to his Barefoot Water-skiing Camp. I
was in. I was not the type to turn down chances for things like
this in life. Opportunity—and savage fun—were knocking and I
was answering the door.

I was flooded with memories of watching barefoot water-skiing at SeaWorld in San Diego when I was a kid. It's walking on water...I felt that this was a sport for me.

I arrived at camp on a Monday afternoon, ready to jump in. Everyone had come well-equipped with booze. A lot of it. Hastily, I made a trip back to the liquor store. I picked up a bottle of Advil, too, just in case.

We feasted and drank like fish. There were eight participants gathered and a coach. Plans were made to head out on the lake at six-thirty a.m. the following morning. The forecast was for rain and a temperature of only six degrees Celsius.

I discussed the learning plan with Coach (never knew him by any other name for six more years). I would learn how to get up forwards and how to do a tumble turn; that means spinning a 360 while sitting on my buttocks. Come afternoon, I would learn how to get up backwards and by the next day I would do a running start off the dock. Going backwards?! You mean, one can ski backwards?

At 6:30 a.m., it was raining and cold, and Coach said I was the first one up. Despite being terribly hung over, I was ready.

Coach instructed me on how to start by gliding on my shoulders, then sitting up on my butt, slowly placing my feet on the water. Then when he sped the boat up, I should slowly stand up.

The boat started going, and now I was trying to remember exactly what he said, and in what order. *Screw it, I'll just figure it out. Stand up and ski.* As the boat started to speed up, I was now sitting on my butt and I figured I was ready to go, so I jammed my feet into the water like a drunk teenager, and *wham*—down I went. I didn't even get a chance to close my eyes before my face hit the water like a ton of bricks. My sinuses were jammed full, and my eyelids needed peeling open to let the extra water out. Maybe, just maybe, this sport was a little harder than I thought it would be. I was swimming in my own cockiness...and the water was freezing.

Coach circled back with the boat. Everyone was laughing hysterically. It was suggested that this time I should try following Coach's directions. No contest there. The epic fail, of course, just happened to be captured on video...

Try number two was a lot smoother. I got up skiing on my feet. What an incredible feeling that is to be flying over the water with no water skis on. Just my bare feet skimming over the surface. I glanced down towards my feet and before I even got to see them, my face was back in the water. This time though, my chin went in first, and my feet came over next. I managed to kick myself in the back of my head. This is called a scorpion. It really is the one fall you don't want to take, as I am pretty sure my spine had never bent like that before, nor should it ever be bent like that again. I learned the first rule of barefooting: "Look down, go down!"

Attempt number three found me following Coach's instructions even more closely and I managed to ski to the end of the lake.

Most of the learning gets done on a bar—or boom—that sticks out the side of the boat. This way the driver can see you, talk to you, and correct the boat speed to help with what you are trying to do. In the learning stages, the make-or-break factor has less to do with the skier, and more to do with the skill of the driver. The Coach doubles as the driver, unlike any other water-ski sport, and a good driver makes the skier look good.

I was wet, succumbing to the cold, and the skies were unleashing upon us. Coach kept telling me to get up and do it again. However, when the shivering starts for me, my learning slows or even stops altogether. But I continued to persevere.

The feeling of skiing across the glassy water on your feet does not have an equal in life in any other sport. Possibly snow skiing in deep powder comes close, but it's not the same. This feels like flying.

Coach declared me a fast learner. He said I should try skiing one-footed. I got up, shifted my weight over the foot I was going to stand on (just like I was told to do), and then yanked my other foot off the water. My foot on the water immediately sank up to my knee. I went cartwheeling down the lake with my head finally penetrating the surface of the water and acting as an anchor to stop the forward motion of my body. I don't think I've ever heard my neck make such nasty noises.

Attempt number two to do a one-foot went a whole lot better...until I got cocksure, and it ended in my second scorpion of the day.

I got back in the boat and wrapped up in a blanket, and shivered and froze for the next hour while my three other friends had their turns on the water. By the time we made it back to the cabin for breakfast, I wasn't sure I'd ever warm up again. This may have been the coldest I'd ever been in my life (but I had not, as of yet, faced The Death Race).

A hot meal and percolated espressos, thankfully, greeted me upon return. There was even a chef there for the week cooking our meals. Everything had been planned for.

The sport was twenty times harder than any sport I had ever learned. The satisfaction I got from very small improvements was incredible. Barefooting requires a high level of precision and flawless technique. I was humbled immediately and repeatedly. Reining in my overly confident self-assuredness was proving to be my biggest challenge at twenty-six.

By the end of the second afternoon, I'd learned how to do the tumble turn and a flying dock start.

By the third morning, I found I couldn't do a sit up to get out of bed. All the muscles from my groin to my chin felt like they had been ripped to shreds and were no longer functioning. The only way to get out of bed was to find a way to roll over onto my stomach and then do a push-up to get my head off the pillow. This was an entirely new level of full-body pain, which, *again,* I had brought entirely upon myself. But I was not alone in the world of ripped muscles and bodily torture, and luckily misery loves company.

By the end of that first week, I was so addicted to the sport that I booked to come back the following year. I love challenges, and this sport was showing that there really was no end to the challenge that it would provide for me.

The next year, Barefoot Camp was better than anything I could have imagined. Coach now knew me well enough to really push me to my limits. I was told getting good at barefooting was not going to happen without a massive dose of intense effort and a constant belief that what I was about to do was going to succeed. Trying something without the belief of success was not worth trying. On many first attempts, Coach would turn the boat around after I fell and tell me to "Go try that like you are going to succeed." This is such a powerful mindset that it became a motto for everything else in life I subsequently applied myself to.

That second year I learned how to turn from backwards to forwards, front toe holds (you put your foot into the handle strap, moving along on one foot while being pulled by your other foot), and skiing backwards on the long rope, along with more one-footed maneuvers.

Nothing compares to the feeling of gliding on water on your feet.
Photo: Roger Cocking

Barefoot suits are made of thick neoprene and are more akin to body armour than a life jacket. This is supposed to protect the skier from the impact on the water, and to keep water out of places that it should not go. This did not always go as planned.

After one grueling, lengthy set of trying to get up on the long rope behind the boat in the very rough water, I found out how porous the suits were. I was standing on the swim platform on the back of the boat, and as I peeled my arms out of the suit, I commented that we must have hit bottom with the boat because there was moss all over the back of the swim platform. Erich, whose boat we were using, took one look at the "moss" and shoved me back into the lake while yelling, "That is not moss!" Apparently, I had an enema in my wetsuit. That "moss" was shit. Sadly, for me, this was on video, and no, you do not get a link to watch the event.

Once you have mastered a trick or technique on the boom, where there is no wake to deal with, you then move to the long rope behind the boat. Now you get to deal with prop wash, turbulence, and nasty wake to cross over. Not only does the difficulty factor more than double, but it also makes it seem like a whole new sport. On the boom, relatively, it feels smooth and serene. On the long rope, it feels like you're being beaten senseless while wrestling a gorilla.

I was getting pretty good at getting up backwards on the boom. Then I tried for three days on the long rope and never fully got up skiing to make it outside the wake and into the smooth, calm water. I came close a few times, but when I eventually made it and skied away in the summer of 1999, I decided that was one of the more well-deserved accomplishments in my sporting life.

There is a saying: "The master has failed more times than the novice has ever tried." I fully understand that now. Barefooting taught me failure over and over again. I had a lot more failures coming my way in barefooting, but for every fall, I made sure I got right back up and did better on the next attempt.

I learned that barefooting competitions existed...and my goal immediately became to become world champion. I told Coach I was dead serious. This was the single greatest addiction in my life. He said he was currently training one of the world's best in Florida, and if I wanted to join them in the fall, I was more than welcome. I seized the opportunity.

It was October 1998 and I was in Winter Haven, Florida, in the "Sunshine State" and the epicenter of barefoot water-skiing. I was in the boat with two of the top instructors in the world, Coach and Lane Bowers. They believed in me as strongly as I did, and they pushed me harder than I ever thought I could be pushed.

I started entering competitions in British Columbia, followed by the United States, and I was given a chance to compete for Canada in the 2001 Pan-American Games in North Dakota. This was the epic stepping-stone I needed, as I now got to meet all the best barefooters in the world.

The Pan-Am Games were a total eye-opener in the world of sport for me. Up to this point in my life, I'd been one of the top snowboarders in the world and had competed in almost every snowboard race that existed. I was a seasoned racer and knew all the head games athletes played with each other. I knew what it took to get in the start gate and mentally beat a competitor who may have been better than me. But I was not ready for what the skiers at a barefoot water-ski competition did...

In this sport, there was comradery. "Competitors" genuinely celebrated with each other, even if displaced from the podium.

If unthroned, the "loser" ran over to the skier who'd beat him and gave him a massive hug and a huge high five. The second-place skier was not bummed about being knocked out of the standings, as he was jubilant that the other person had thrown down the best run of their life and beat him. This happened over and again and again. I'd never seen this before, and I didn't really know what to make of it at first. It was only then it dawned on me that every one of these barefooters were friends. Everyone here knew how damned hard it was to get to this point of competition and what it took in practice to get to that level. They were always excited when a friend pulled off an amazing run! This kind of comradery took a bit to get used to for me, as snowboard racing had never been like this.

By the end of the Pan-Am Games, I hadn't just boosted my confidence and my skill set, but I now knew I was being supported by a hundred new barefooters who cared that I did my best on the competition day.

There are three different events in the barefooting discipline, and most athletes compete in all three events.

In the slalom event, competitors get a fifteen-second run down the lake, where they are scored for each crossing of the wake that is made. Competitors receive a single point for doing it on one-foot crosses and a half-point for doing so on two feet. You are then given a second pass on the way back down the lake. On the second pass you get half points if you are going the same direction as the first pass (forwards or backwards skiing) and full points if you choose to ski it the opposite way. The boat moves at forty-seven mph for this event.

The trick event is also based on a fifteen-second run. The goal is to do as many different tricks in that time as possible. You get two passes down the lake, and there are no points for repeated tricks. Each trick has its own point value based on its difficulty. A list of the tricks includes: one foots, toeholds, tumble turns, flips, 180s, 360s, 720s, and line steps.

Then there is the jumping event. The jump is eight feet long, eighteen inches high, and thirty-six inches wide. The goal is to jump as far as possible after going over the ramp at forty-three mph. There are two different techniques employed. The hard part is just keeping your balance, as the ramp is polished fiberglass and is slipperier than the water.

The first, or the traditional jumping method, has a skier going over the ramp in the upright position, and as you gain lift from the ramp the upright position is maintained through the air. The landing occurs as the feet come down first, contact the water, and then usually absorb the landing on the butt and then back up to the feet. It's considered a successful jump if you can be back in the basic barefooting position before a specified run-out distance after the ramp.

Then there is inverted jumping. Using this method, a skier rides up the ramp, pushes off more aggressively, and allows their feet to be pushed up, flattening their body in the air. The skier then looks like superman flying through the air while up to twelve feet over the water, and at forty-three mph. The hard part of this technique is getting the timing to work out so that they get their feet back down to impact the water to cushion the landing. This is a rather spectacular event, strictly due to the horrific crashes that occur when things go wrong, and on many days, they go wrong more often than they go right.

I spent months and months training for inverted jumping. Coach even gave me a jump as a wedding present. Hours upon hours of jumping and crashing and trying again filled my summers.

I was so addicted that I purchased a jump in Florida, where I was training, so that I could attain the inverted jumping.

I trained using the boom out the side of the boat and went to a longer and longer rope as I progressed. The crashes were horrible. After a while I was starting to think that I was in one long bout of concussion recovery. Crashing from twelve feet in the air at forty-three mph is debilitating. Especially when you need to get back up, do it again, and not make the same mistake.

Inverted jumping ended up being my nemesis in the sport. Try as I might, I was unable to convince my body to do the inverted jump when I transferred to the long rope behind the boat. Maybe I had taken too many nasty crashes, or maybe it was the lingering PTSD from the helicopter crash that I had so far been ignoring and covering up. All I knew was that when I tried to jump inverted, my brain would not allow me to do what was needed.

Eventually, I abandoned the idea of obtaining the inverted jumping skill—I would have to move on without it. This was a rotten feeling of knowing I should be able to do it, but something inside of me was resisting. It was a major indicator in my life that I did have lingering traumas and would one day have to deal with them. At that point, though, I was not ready to deal with the demons.

By the time I was thirty, I was competing in the seniors category. *Seriously.* It's a very young man's sport. I don't know any other sport where you are considered old at this age, but since there's more potential for associated injuries, youth does hold many advantages.

I realized that taking six months off barefooting each winter to stay in Whistler and work made it challenging to stay in top form. To circumvent this issue, I went to Florida for a week each spring and fall. This way I could train more and prep myself as well as possible for the upcoming season. Florida was also where the best barefooters in the world spent their time on the water, so I thought I should spend some time training with them.

Some days when I trained with Coach, I couldn't decide if he was trying to squeeze the best out of me or just trying to kill me in the process. I think one of his training methods was to ski through any water condition while always maintaining balance. It is very common in Florida to ski along the edge of the lakes where we are only a couple feet away from the weeds. This was where the smoothest water often was. This also gave Coach the chance to drive through the weeds while I was skiing backwards on the boom. We would go farther and farther into the weeds, with Coach laughing hysterically until I eventually fell. Coach would then be sitting in the boat out in the lake, reminding me that the weedy areas are where the alligators like to live.

It is said that to become a professional in a sport, you'll need 10,000 hours of practice. This is the hard part for barefooting, as it really is hard to get out on the water for hours of training each day, especially if you end up taking a few nasty crashes. The average pass down a lake is about thirty seconds, and that's if you have a big lake. An average set on the water may give you up to eight passes. You rarely train alone, so it is then likely that you will have to give way for another skier in the boat to train. Your next attempt may not be for another hour or more. Then there are the water conditions and weather, which factor greatly into scheduling—from stormy waters to the unpredictability of inner tubes and other boaters. Plus, in Canada, ice is on the lake longer than it is off.

To get to the 10,000 hours to be a professional, I figured it took me a little more than fifteen years. The sport galvanized my spirit and passion...from a local through to world level.

A LIFE WITH SCARS

I WAS WEARING A FULL-FACE MASK AND A FOAM NECK collar, and my fresh facial scars were bright red under the protective plastic shield. I did not look "normal." Most people stared at me in stark disbelief—at times, repulsed—as they had never seen another human in this condition, let alone one that was out walking and talking. To say I was lucky to have good friends was a total understatement.

My friends wouldn't let me be "different." They wouldn't exclude me from anything, and they certainly were not going to let me sit around and feel sorry for myself. I drew in amazing energy and a sense of power from them. I knew I could not let them, or myself, down. I made a point of going out into the world with confidence, self-assurance, and a solid belief that I was still an amazing person underneath...it was just scars on the surface that visually made me appear different.

Every day I told myself that the mask was important, and it was going to be the primary tool in my road to healing. I believed this with all my heart. I recited this idea to myself every day. I had to believe that the mask was necessary, otherwise the following years of wearing it would have broken me. By believing in the mask, I was able to believe in my own self when out in public and not feel embarrassed or ashamed.

The face mask was both a blessing and a curse.

During those -30ºC days, while snowboarding, I remember coming in from the cold a few times and realizing that the mask would not come off. It had frozen to my face. I imagine that probably wasn't so good for the skin, but it managed to keep the red colour out of the scars. At least until it thawed out.

On the flip side, the plastic did not offer any sun protection, so I had to put on sunscreen under the mask every day. This kept my skin moist; however, when I sweated, the mask would just go milky white. It looked exactly as you just pictured it.

The big problem with new scars is that if they get too much sun, then the pigment gets destroyed and the scar will remain dark-brown and blotchy forever, which is why I was so adamant about sunscreen. All day, every day, I applied it. I'm pretty sure that I've been so genetically modified that my children probably won't ever need to use it.

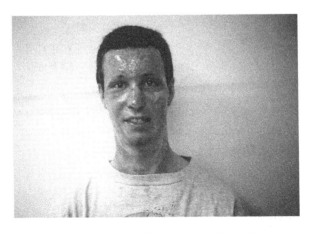

The scars were bright red for many years. Photo: Mom

Eating posed the greatest challenge. Generally, I wore a ball cap to cover up the straps that went around my head, holding the mask in place. I'll admit, oddly, I was a bit self-conscious about things like that, but was just fine with the mask and the scars. When I would eat and chew, I had to remove the mask. So off would come the hat and the mask, and then I'd need to wipe my face and get the slimy sunscreen off, and then I was ready to eat. By this time, if I was in a restaurant, all the diners were now staring at me with a look suggesting that I had just destroyed their appetite. Fortunately, I did not care, nor did my friends I was dining with. There were some advantages to being in my twenties and believing the world revolved around me.

It was not always an easy road. Everywhere I went while wearing that plastic mask, people would stare at me. Some in disgust. Some in disbelief. Some in awe. Some with confusion. Some were just stunned. A few even had a curious look and were quite interested in exactly what I was wearing, along with why, and how it would help me. This last group of people were few and far between.

Kids, at least, were honest—their innocence compelling. They would just look at their parents and ask why that man was wearing a mask, or why his face was red. I loved listening to the replies, as responses were so varied. Only once, or twice, did the parents respond to their child by saying that they should go and ask me. And then the child would. Those were some of the best conversations I ever had. Children are so open and honest that I really think adults would do quite well to take lessons from their kids.

Children are normally full of curiosity and wonder. They ask great questions, fully accept the answer, and are not hiding behind any false fronts or trying to show off to their buddies. Kids are brutally honest, and it always made my day when I talked to them about burns, scars, fire, and healing. Quite often, I told them that this is what happens to you if you play with matches and fire in your house. The look on their faces would always tell me if they had done so before and had been fortunate to have not burnt their house down. I am pretty sure that the eavesdropping parents were appreciative of those comments—as I'm sure their kids never forgot them.

Adults, on the other hand, can be...well, angels or assholes. Every day, people tested every facet of my patience, tolerance, good nature, and self-control. Rude comments, disgusted looks, parents shielding their children from a freak, and just general treatment as though I was a total aberration, were not uncommon. Many days I just accepted that I was set upon the world to be challenged. Way too many times I had people tell me that God only gave people challenges that they could deal with. I believe in a lot of things, but a God that would do that to a person is not one of them.

The most common reaction was the long, blank stare. People would see me from a distance, then be unable to take their eyes off me until I had walked well out of sight. On more than one occasion I heard people comment to their buddies about the freak they'd just seen, and then run back around to get a better look. This was akin to being kicked square in the nuts.

I did learn to ignore those things, to try to not let them affect me. I was able to walk through Whistler Village and my friends would ask how I dealt with so many people staring at me. I would have no clue what they were referring to, as I had been walking around with blinders on, and I really hadn't seen them.

This is not a good way to go through life, as you will then miss out on everything else that is positive. You may also miss spotting the bear on the side of the trail that you just walked by. Yes, that happened to me, as Whistler is full of bears.

I remember when a friend was very concerned about how people were looking at us, and I said that they were not looking at me, it was him. I told him he had barbecue sauce on his face and wine on his shirt and he looked like a dirtbag. The look of shock on his face was priceless as he tried to clean off the non-existent sauce and couldn't find any wine on his dark shirt.

For four years I wore that face mask.

I received a first-hand, in-depth education on human nature. I learned how to determine who someone is within seconds.

Did they look me in the eye? Were they curious? Were they just trying to look cool in front of their friends? Were they just a jerk and trying to somehow prove they were better than me? Were they in the medical field and had never seen the plastic mask before? Did they feel sorry for me? What level of compassion did they have? These became the things I could determine within the first ten seconds of engaging with someone, and this skill has stayed with me since. For this, I am ever grateful.

On a few occasions my mom and I got into some deep conversations about how it was probably a good thing that it was me who got burned and not some other people we knew. The reasoning was that we were pretty sure if it had happened to a lot of these others, it would have totally ruined their lives, whereas I seemed to be doing a pretty good job of piecing myself back together. I really do not know how true that would be, as most people have no idea what they are capable of until they are tested and then find out. I would like to think that most people would step their game up to the occasion, but I also think many would be completely ruined by such an occurrence. Hopefully you will never have to find out who you really are in this way, and what you are capable of. It is not as liberating as you might think it would be. Knowing is nice but experiencing it sucks.

I was not always honest when people asked me what had happened to me. Some days, I just had to entertain myself. I relayed stories of fighter planes or what-have-you...it depended on who was asking and why. I had to find the fun. Usually, I just made up part of whatever story was in the news. On more than a few occasions I waded deep into a story about how my fighter jet had flamed out over Iraq and how I had walked for days to get to safety. I'm sure they believed me, or at least they wanted to believe it was true.

Some people I encountered were so rude that I could not bother to muster a response to them. It often seemed that my friends had a much stronger reaction to these people than I did. Probably because I was used to that kind of treatment, and it was not conceivable to my friends that people could act that way.

While at a snowboard race in Mt. Baker, WA, I was at a big dinner party at one of the local bars. I was chatting with one of the local girls and having a beer, when an obviously intoxicated man came up and made a horribly disparaging comment towards me and the mask I was wearing. I shrugged it off as the guy was drunk, and he probably would not have said such a thing if he had thought about it more. As I turned away from him, I heard the meaty slap of a fist striking face, and then the sound of a body dropping to the floor. When I turned around, there was the rude guy lying face down on the floor in a puddle of beer and dirt with the girl I'd been talking to standing over him, rubbing her fist.

When I asked her what happened, she said that she could not believe how rude he was, and that she had hit him. She said she had been nice and turned her ring around backwards so that it wouldn't peel his face open. She could not believe how easily he'd dropped, as she exclaimed that she hadn't hit him all that hard. I still get reminded by my friends about how the girls take care of my fights for me.

It was events such as that where I was reminded that the scars were going to be with me for a long time. Figuring out how to accept them and move on was going to be vital for my future. The scars might fade over time, but they would be a part of me for the rest of my life, and they were certainly going to shape me into a new person whether I wanted to be that person or not. This was going to be my life forevermore, and the sooner I accepted it, the better.

Growing up as a white male in Canada certainly comes with its privileges, and rarely do we ever get a chance to see what life would be like if we did not have that privilege. Going through life with highly visible facial scars suddenly put me in one of the smallest visible minority groups out there. It really has given me a great understanding of others and what challenges they may be going through from being different. I would say I am now quite fortunate to have lived in society as two very different people: a privileged white male and a visible minority.

My real friends do not notice the scars, as they do not treat me any differently, and they still hold me accountable for everything I do. They are the true heroes in the world, as I unfortunately have discovered there are certainly not enough people like this.

Early on, when the scars were intensely red, I often wondered how I would ever have a girlfriend again. I really was not a stunning beauty to look at, that's for sure.

The first girl that seemed really interested in me that first summer asked one night how I could kiss with the mask on. When I said that I could take it off, her eyes lit up, and my heart swelled a thousand-fold! In order to kiss, I would have to take off the mask, then wipe off the moisture cream. I was very aware of what this must have smelled like. After that, when she still wanted to kiss me, I cannot possibly convey what a boost this was to my confidence!

Prior to going to sleep, I needed to put the nylon, full-face, Jobst garment back on and I looked like Mr. Potato Head. Women must have seen more in me than I could possibly have known. The procedure was a lot for me to deal with, let alone someone I was intimate with.

Every day during that time, I found I had to repeat to myself that the mask was needed. It was the key to my recovery. This was a personal mantra, a rallying cry. The scars would eventually become okay, I assured myself, I just needed to front-load the necessary work. It would be easier to do it myself *now*, than face more surgeries later. At the end of the first year, I went back to Calgary to check in with the physiotherapy clinic. We spoke about scars, healing, and life for a very long time. At the end of that discussion, we decided that the best thing for my scars would be to wear the mask for another year.

The scars were improving rapidly. I was dedicated and committed to wearing the mask, as was instructed. I knew that if I was to leave the mask off for an hour, then it would really be the equivalent to setting myself back a day. And, if for some reason I left it off for a whole night, then that would be like negating the previous month of wearing it. Knowing this was vital in my process, I never went to sleep without it on—*ever*.

Every three or four months I would go back to the physio-therapy clinic in Calgary, and we would build a new mask. This process involved taking a rubberized mold of my face and then making a plaster cast from it, then shaping the plastic over the plaster cast. The plaster would then be shaved down in specific areas so that we could gain more pressure over specific pieces of scar tissue. Finally, a new plastic mask was made from the modified plaster.

Scars age at different rates, and some of the thicker scars needed more pressure to stay flat on my face. Scars also mature better when they are pressed firmly and evenly, as this prevents any keloid effect. The mask did wonders for this.

During this time, I also started to reshape my nose. Two months before the helicopter crash, I had fallen into a ditch on Whistler Mountain, smashed my knees into my face, and peeled my nose almost completely off my face. When it was stitched back on, and healed up, it was quite crooked. During the time wearing the mask, I reset my nose back to where it should have been! This was cheap—literal plastic—surgery, as far as I could tell!

Rebuilding of some of my face was also part of the process. I was missing my left eyebrow, and a couple of the scars on my lip were also large and thick. I never understood why we have eyebrows, until I no longer had one. Every time I sweated or was in the shower, the water would run down in my eye. I now have a whole new appreciation as to why hair grows on our bodies where it does.

One day of surgery was cutting out an eyebrow-shaped piece of my scalp from the back of my head and stitching it back in place as my new eyebrow. This was all done with local freezing.

The sound of the scalpel cutting out chunks of flesh from my head is not something I want to experience again, especially as cutting through tough scar tissue takes quite a bit of force. The surgeon did an amazing job, as my eyebrow looks as normal as can be.

At the end of year two, I had another meeting with the physiotherapy team in Calgary. Again, we spoke of scars, healing, and life. Again, at the end of our discussion, we decided that the best thing for my scars was to wear the mask for another year. At first it was a shock, but I was able to absorb this information quickly, as the mask had taught me, above anything else, resilience.

The scars continued to mature well. Each month they became less and less red and stayed flatter longer and longer when I took the mask off.

And at the end of the third year, when I returned to Calgary to discuss getting rid of the mask, the discussion led to me wearing it for a fourth year. What was one more year going to be, after I had already done three? At that point, it just did not make any difference to me. The mask was so ingrained into my life, that I almost would not know what to do without it.

There were some great advantages to wearing the mask. Admittedly, I had to dig deep to find these, but I did. When I went mountain biking through the bush, no branches hit me in the face. When I flew, the flight attendants often gave me an upgrade and served me the good wine. It worked at least sixty percent of the time, so I thought it to be a pretty good bonus. For Halloween, I always had the best costume. On a couple of occasions, I dressed up as the two-face guy from the comics. One year I took an old mask, drew felt-tip marker lines all over it, and then heated up nails and poked them through the mask. I turned into Hellraiser. That was probably one of the better uses of the old masks.

For Halloween I always used my scars to my advantage.

Living a life with scars brought me full circle to the Burn Fund in Vancouver in 2015. I was the guest speaker for the night, and I was trying to bring up the subject of all the good things that having been a burn survivor has brought me. I talked about how it made me who I am, and how it had molded my life for the past thirty years. I said that if I had it to do all over again, I wouldn't want to change a thing.

One man told his story about how the propane bottle blew up in the back of his motorhome while he was driving and how he lost his fingers in the fire. He had been trapped in his seat by the seat belt while the whole vehicle was going up in flames. He was only a few months out of the burn ward, and it looked like he had another fifteen years of surgeries and skin grafts ahead of him. Compared to him, I had barely burnt my tongue on a hot cup of coffee.

He went on to say how his life was so much better now and how he was eternally grateful for the fire. The fire had ended his life of drugs and alcohol and given him the opportunity to rekindle a relationship with his children. He explained that he was now close with his mother for the first time in his life and that it had brought his whole family back together.

I arrived home and immediately told my wife and children about the world's most amazing man. I explained how everything that ever happens to you can be seen as a good thing. It may not seem that way initially, but eventually you will draw the positive from it. If a man who had been burnt near to death and was facing a life of pain could believe it, then so could we. We should never find reason to complain about anything ever again.

Every day presented me with a new challenge, and not always one that I was ready for. Every person I met gave me a new experience, and not always the experience I would have liked. I did, however, surround myself with supportive, non-judgmental, and fabulously loving people...making every day all that much more rewarding. The scars and mask created these challenges and experiences, molding not only my face, but also my personality. I am forever grateful for these life lessons, showing me the impossible is possible.

THE WORLD'S TOUGHEST MUDDER

THE RAT PACK. THAT'S THE NAME THAT KEN LUBIN, PJ Rakowski and I were given during the 2010 Death Race. It was a great name, in our opinion, and we became known by it for several years.

After having a three-way tie for first at the 2013 Death Race (my third), we somehow talked ourselves into testing our limits one more time. The next logical step was the World's Toughest Mudder.

The World's Toughest Mudder is quite a different event from the Death Race. In this event, you know everything about the course ahead of time. This was going to be a totally new experience for us. Our common question, if not fear, was: will this be too much information?

What our Rat Pack did have this time was Benjamin. Benjamin: my initial Death Race instigator. For this, he was able to join. This was going to be a bucketload of fun.

The World's Toughest Mudder is twenty-four-hours long. It takes place over a five-mile course with twenty-five obstacles. There was only one self-imposed catch: we would run as a team, always to be within a hundred metres of each other for the duration. If one person dropped out, we all would drop out.

Benjamin had been through Army Ranger training, Ken had an un-godly pain tolerance, and PJ never fatigued. I knew my level of fitness and what I had done for training, but my challenge was going to be running. I was not a distance runner. I could carry one hundred pounds for a month, but at a walking pace. The running part was going to tax my abilities.

The race was in New Jersey, in the middle of November. The potential for cold was almost certain. The course was mostly mud and obstacles where if you failed, you ended up in water. We would be running in wetsuits and cold for the entire period of the race. I was already envisioning, much to my disgust, what our bodies would look like after twenty-four-hours in a wetsuit.

An outside temperature of five degrees Celsius greeted us as we arrived at the track in Jersey. First thing we did was set up our support base at the event site. Every five miles we passed that point where we could restock food and water or rest, if needed. We chose to put down a tarp to stay out of the mud, and we had four lawn chairs and a stocked cooler (burger, butter, the usual). It seemed like everyone else had tents. Did they know something we did not?

We asked around about the shelters. The response was so that competitors could get some sleep during the night. Sleep?! This was a short race. We could, and would, sleep after. We didn't want to compromise our competitive edge with post-nap craggi-ness. This was about winning. Sleep was for the losers.

Stories were circulating. Other teams were talking about the Rat Pack, and how they were the ones to beat. We, of course, asked to have them pointed out so we would know our competi-tion, but nobody seemed to know what they looked like. Our reputation was preceding us. Our previous Death Race and

Ultra Beast wins (yes, another race, another story...another chapter—actually, more appropriately, a sequel...) were becoming the things of legend. We were hearing some incredible, death-defying stories about what we had supposedly done. The exaggerations were quite funny.

One story I coerced out of a racer was about how the Rat Pack had sprinted the entire twenty-six miles of the Ultra Beast the year before. Apparently, the legends were growing. We had only sprinted to pass another team to crush their spirits and have them stop trying so hard. The mental game was what we were good at.

The 2013 World's Toughest Mudder was composed of over a thousand competitors, with thirty teams, coming from every corner of the world.

The sun poked its head out for the start of the race.

Lap one had us soaking wet, cold, and excited. We opted to do it without wetsuits, figuring we could put them on after if we really needed them. We ran it quite casually, having a good look at all the obstacles along the way and prepping plans on how to get us through them as a team. On the first lap, most of the obstacles were not used so that the 1000-person field could stretch out and there would not be a lineup to use the obstacles. The seriously daunting-looking element was Electric Shock.

The Tough Mudder is widely known for naming its obstacles, and the notoriously feared, electrified obstacle is usually at the very end. It has all manner of dangly wires suspended over the water, and they are charged with ludicrous amounts of electricity, which grounds out in the muddy puddles under your feet. When the body gets hit by one of these wires, it feels like you have been struck by a lightning bolt. The last time I was hit by one, my arm went numb and I convulsed like a leaf in a hurricane. It is always at the end of the course, so I would get to think about the shock for the entire run around the course.

On lap number two, the field was stretched out significantly, and it was time to hit all the obstacles. The first was the mud bog, a 500-metre trough of waist-deep mud, with four-foot-high walls of clay sticking out. With no foot or hand holds, we assisted each other in getting over every one of these walls, and there were ten of them.

By the time we got out of the mud, every place on our bodies (as well as our gear) was plugged full of heavy clay. Our shoes, which were light to start with, were now cement. There just isn't time to stop, as there will always be another mud bog coming up within a few hundred metres.

We were challenged by Walk the Plank. While climbing to the top of the tower, we had plenty of time to think about what was coming. There was a ten-inch-wide plank sticking six feet out past the top of the tower. Fifteen feet below was a thick crash pad sitting in a giant cargo net. The only problem was we would have to jump at least eight feet across the empty span to land on the net. Otherwise, it was eight metres to the mud bog below.

We had to run out onto the plank and launch ourselves into space, then try to land softly onto the crash pad after a fifteen-foot drop. I still had a nagging fear of heights at this point (though that has yet to ever be mentioned, it's true: a ski-guide-cum-heli-pilot made scared by rising elevation), so this was really taxing the adrenals every time I anticipated it.

PJ, Ben, and I all made it without disaster; but we couldn't see Ken. Finally, we spotted him off to the side, with his shoulder obviously dislocated. That was not good. One man out, the whole team was out. He had told us before the race that he was going in for surgery a couple weeks after the race to fix his shoulder, and we'd just chosen to ignore this problem up until that point.

Ken coached us on how to put his shoulder back into its socket, and after immediate relief from the pain, he said he was ready to continue. We took him at his word and off we went.

Six. That is the number of times that Ken dislocated his shoulder on the first lap. We kept putting it back in, and he continued to keep popping it back out. The focus from there on in was figuring out how to get Ken over each obstacle without his shoulder dislocating.

By the end of lap number four, with twenty miles of running under our shoes, we had now sorted out how to get over each obstacle. Ken's shoulder stayed intact. We heard we were in second place in the team event. The group that was in front of us was a batch of military college twenty-somethings.

Lap five had us running in wetsuits. It was getting dark, and it was getting cold. We were anticipating freezing overnight. We had been cold before and did not die, so we thought this shouldn't be a big deal.

What was a big deal was knowing exactly how long we had left in the race. We also knew exactly what we were going to encounter on every lap. This became mental torture. Knowing what was coming, and when, just made the anticipation of it worse and worse, every lap. Knowing too much was starting to haunt us. The unexpected nature of the Death Race served as fuel, but in contrast, the relentless repetition of The World's Toughest Mudder was deflating. Like most things in life, the anticipation of the obstacle or event is often worse than the event itself

By the middle of the night, the Walk the Plank was becoming downright terrifying. The night was just barely illuminated by our tiny head lamps. We were launching ourselves into the dark abyss, knowing that there was going to be a massive impact into the crash pad down in the cargo net. Our bodies were aching, sore, and tired. Everything hurt.

Walk the Plank was nasty, but it was nothing compared to hitting Shock Therapy. Shock Therapy started out with a trivia question, and depending on which answer you chose, it took you down a different path. This version of Shock Therapy had us crawling under barbed wire, with the little dangly wires hanging down all over the place. It was not possible to get through without touching the wires; however, all the wires were not charged all the time. It was hit-and-miss.

Shock Therapy wires at the Tough Mudder. My favourite. Photo: Tough Mudder

When we got the random trivia question correct, the shock wires were not charged at all. A wrong answer meant you got blasted. There was one story rolling around where a racer got knocked unconscious by the shock and had to be dragged out of the obstacle by his buddy. This did not sound good. In fact, it was downright scary. It was amazing how much I psyched myself up for the electroshock each lap. I'd had no idea how much I disliked being electrocuted at random. Or maybe I was just absolutely pissed off that we had gotten the trivia question wrong.

By the tenth lap, all my brain could focus on was the hope we would get the trivia question right. Every other obstacle now felt simple in comparison. We had come up with the wrong answer too many times, and the shocks had just about paralyzed me. The World's Toughest Mudder had found my weakness and was attacking me like lemon juice on a paper cut.

By two a.m., we had a routine: survive the lap with Ken's shoulder intact. Pray that we would get the trivia question correct. Make it back to the pit and have a litre of hot soup, fat-bar concoctions, and put on fresh socks. Then we would alternate each lap between a Red Bull and 800 mg of Advil. Pain relief was an exceptional benefit, and Red Bull did what Red Bull does. If you have never had a Red Bull before, it really is like taking a massive dose of adrenalin, and it acts like a powerful mental stimulant. I do not like sugar, but the mental kick-in-the-pants seemed to be what was needed. Anything that boosted my spirit while I was fearing the electric shock was good. The Death Race has taught me that the mental state I am in is all important when it comes to success.

Being extremely cold and having to get up and run constantly is a mental challenge like none other. If I walked, then my body did not hurt, but I was horrifically cold. When I ran, at least I warmed up, but then my body screamed at me like it was being tortured. Suddenly, those people who were taking naps looked darned smart. That was not why we were there, though. We kept going.

The Rat Pack. Twenty-four hours in, the wetsuit was a special kind of miserable.
Photo: Alison Armstrong Lubin

We did not know it, but we were only ten minutes behind the military boys for most of the race. Talking with them after the event was quite entertaining, as they gave up some of their secrets. They had purposefully positioned people all over the course to act as spies and keep an eye on our Rat Pack. They said the hardest part for them was that we never stopped for long breaks in the pits. They, too, would only stop in for two or three minutes, and then would have to scramble to keep ahead of us. I was happy to hear that we were their biggest concern in the race. It's good to know that the old guys made those young kids work hard for the win.

Daylight was starting to light up the course, and we could finally ditch the headlamps. We had four more hours to go, and Ken hadn't dislocated his shoulder for at least three laps.

The constant cold and the need to wear gloves during the night caused my fingers to lose feeling. Gripping the monkey bars was not an option, so I jumped straight into the water trap and swam across. It was not pretty, but it got the job done. Like golf, there was no room on the scorecard for pictures or comments.

I remember a great motivational sign on the course that read: "Pain is temporary, but internet race results are forever." This thought remained in the back of my head, right next to the memory of quitting the Death Race in 2012. That deep, dark place that I never wanted to return to...*ever*. The memory of the *16x9* documentary followed me everywhere. It was a constant reminder of how I said I would never quit, and then I did.

Fourteen laps into the event and seventy miles later, we were pretty sure that the army kids were only five minutes in front of us. We had a plan. A fast pitstop to knock back two Red Bulls and another handful of Advil, and we were back on the course in less than a minute.

Fully jacked up and fortified, the plan was to sprint down the one-mile racetrack and put up a chase. Once we had them in our sights, we would overtake them on Walk the Plank. This was going to be awesome!

What actually happened looked nothing like that plan at all. After twenty metres of sprinting, we realized that our idea was not working. Not a single body part was willing to cooperate. The brain was convinced it would work, but the body parts went on strike. We looked at each other, shrugged our shoulders, and continued at a different pace. It more closely resembled a fast zombie shuffle than anything else. But we were determined to finish that last lap no matter what.

Seventy-five miles of obstacle-chasing hell later, the finish line was in sight. We had gone sixty-five hours in the Death Race, but this seemed a whole lot harder. Knowing all along what was coming up caused a mental battle that I had not been ready for. Going around the same five-mile course fifteen times was undeniably grueling and monotonous, for an otherwise epic experience. This was a mental challenge that we had never encountered before.

While hanging around waiting for the awards to start, we chose to stay in our wetsuits, as we did not know if we had the ability to peel them off and stay warm after. The organizers asked if there was anything that we needed while we were waiting. There was a unanimous decision that above all else, we needed a beer. It was nine a.m., and we were thirsty. Luckily, they brought us several. We were happy.

We landed a third-place trophy, and a cheque for five grand. The money was nice, but we'd had no idea there was another team out there in front of us. How we missed it—*them*—I will never know, but it's those oddball happenings that create the best memories and mysteries.

Waddling back to our hotel, we laughed constantly about all the shenanigans from the past twenty-four hours. We weighed our shoes and found that they were slightly over eight pounds each. No wonder the idea of sprinting the last lap didn't work. They went straight into the garbage can. The stench of the wetsuit coming off is something I am hoping to forget.

I consider this as one of my bigger athletic successes. Running seventy-five miles was not something I ever thought I could do, let alone adding in obstacles, mud, water, and with a teammate's dislocated shoulders.

What I found most shocking from this event was how long it took me to recover physically. After the Death Races, it would take me a couple weeks of healing blisters, mending sore muscles, and being ready to hit the gym. After the WTM, it was three months. From wearing tight neoprene gloves for the whole race, I lost the feeling in my fingertips for a month. Every week I tested my body to see if I was ready to exercise, but the body was not willing. I was fatigued. Constantly. As far as I could tell, my entire metabolic system had shut down. This was a terrifying experience. I tried every method I had in my arsenal to get my body back on-line, with little to no advancement. In the end, it was sleep that restored me. I started sleeping a minimum of eight hours a night, and that finally provided success. It was terrifying having my body out of commission and not knowing why.

The World's Toughest Mudder was an incredible experience in life, and it taught me much. Taking advantage of all the opportunities that have come my way has been a monumental piece of creating who I am. I wouldn't change these experiences for anything in the world. The World's Toughest Mudder gave me yet another chance in life to find out exactly what I was capable of.

This race wasn't just impossible, it was worse. And I loved it.

THE DEATH RACE—SUCCESS

A YEAR'S WORTH OF TRAINING TO GET READY WAS THE WAY I was looking at things as I signed up for the Death Race for a third time in 2013. This go-around, I was fired up and determined to win. Every aspect of my life now turned towards Death Race preparation. I had a one-hundred-pound slam ball, an article in the local newspaper, the Global television documentary had aired, and my mental attitude was as good as it was going to get. All I had to do now was make my training so miserably hard that the race would seem like vacation.

It was the Global TV show *16x9* that had showcased me in the Death Race the year before. It had aired on national TV a few months after the event, and it highlighted the fact that I'd quit. This was a constant kick in the nuts every time I thought about it and how I had talked about winning the event beforehand and proceeded to quit. So, 2013 was about saving face. My ego had taken a beating, and I was on the hunt for redemption.

Nobody would join with me on my training workouts. I have good friends—extreme, adrenalin-sport-chasing friends—but even they told me they were friends, not idiots.

I was working as a ski guide throughout the winter. Mornings, therefore, began at five a.m., crawling around in icy mountain creeks, heaving logs, and hoisting boulders. Alone. I forced myself to find the fun in it all, and I did.

A 100-lb slam ball. What more could a person want for Christmas?
Photo: Lee Schwartz

The month prior to the race, I worked at adding ten pounds of body fat. With my physiology and level of activity, this is much harder than you may think. I was training hard, helping my kids with their dance show (you should see my pirouettes), bucking cords of wood, hauling heavy loads, and wearing my weighted vest. I had to add two extra-large meals every day in order to add the body fat I now knew I'd require. I would lose it entirely—and rapidly—over the duration of the Death Race.

Race day came, and I was ready. Another fifty pounds of necessities, plus this time: a tuxedo! It was the year of "The Gambler." I was convinced we would have to don our tails and have to do the race 007-Bond-style. Sadly, I was disappointed. Although I did sit down and memorize all the words to the song "The Gambler."

Christian, for the third year in succession, was my support crew. This guy was mandatory.

In the forty-eight hours prior to the race, rumours were running rampant. The latest story was that everyone needed to arrive a day early at the farm to work, in order to earn a gambling token needed to finish the race. Competitors were scrambling. I recognized this as a piece of the game, nothing but smoke and mirrors. I was correct, fortunately, and my gambling paid off. By start time—this year at nine a.m.—it was announced that the organizer's casino had gone bankrupt, and all their chips collected the day before were worthless. This kind of trickery makes the race so much more exciting for me. If I was running the show, I would have indulged in the pleasure of doing the same thing.

Registration was listed as beginning at six a.m. and running through to nine. Ken, PJ, and I arrived precisely at 8:59. This turned out to be a very wise decision, as those who had shown up at six were on their second trip of carrying rocks up to the top of the mountain or doing menial farm labour for the past three hours. They were punished for showing up early—but not us.

The first twenty-four hours was spent in group activities. The beatdown portion. In groups of fifteen, we were tasked to build a 1000-vertical-foot stone staircase in the mountainside out of 1000-pound sandstone slabs that had been haphazardly deposited trailside by an excavator. We were informed that the following morning, each group would be forced to vote out one person. It would be the person thought to not be working hard enough. More head games. I knew, from experience, that the only way you were going to be tossed out of the race was if you were either broken or you quit. Even the cheaters just got punished and were allowed to continue. The chance of being voted out by others was just a ruse and not something to be concerned about. I wasn't. Others, evidently, were.

When the sun came up, I was still around and had busied myself during the night by transplanting ferns from the forest to the sides of the staircase. Aesthetics count. We had moved some massive rocks to build our section of the stairs, but I thought it should look nice too. The ferns added a nice touch.

People put in massive amounts of effort to move giant rocks, through a night of screaming, yelling, and outright monstrous physical effort. I was not one of those. This year, I was here for the race, and I was going to win. This part, I knew, was not part of the "racing." I did my part, but there was no point in having a one-ton slab of sandstone land on my foot and take me out of the race.

During the night, we were ordered to lie on the ground, motionless, and not get up for an hour. We were told that anyone who got up, or talked, would be disqualified (another idle threat). I did as I was told, made a bed out of dry leaves, put on my warm clothes, laid down, and slept for an hour. Delightful. I believe the organizer's intent was to have us lie down, get stiff and sore, and not want to get up again. That plainly failed on me. As a parent, I had spent years with my children getting only one hour of sleep a night. I had learned to harness that precious one hour of sleep, and it served to fully recharge me. The race was playing to my strengths now.

I met up with PJ and Ken. Here we were, shuttling ten buckets of gravel up a steep incline. We were all in great spirits. Ken told me a story about some slacker that was planting ferns on the side of the trail last night instead of moving massive rocks! I almost died laughing and had to tell him it was me. That made it even funnier, and luckily, they saw the humour in it, too.

Crawling under barbed wire that was strung over a steep, nasty creek full of large boulders and frigid cold water, and covered with a crisscrossed jumble of snarled logs, came next. With gambling as the prevailing theme, we had to make our way through the nastiness, go to the bottom extreme of the creek, get a playing card from a marshal, who just happened to be Joe Desena's son, then scramble our way back to the top and play a game of high/low. We had to do this until we won the game. On my first five trips up and down, I received a two or a three for my cards, while, funnily enough, the dealer always had an ace. Amazing coincidence. I had come to assume things like this would occur, so it didn't surprise me.

On my sixth trip, I convinced the dealer to let me choose my own card and I found a queen in the deck. Aha! Now I was getting somewhere. Then all I had to do was find a way to get the dealer at the top to play a different card, and I might be done with the barbed wire. At the top, I made a deal with the dealer. I proposed that if I could pick his card from the deck and I won, then I could move on. If I lost, it would cost me two hundred burpees. (As burpees don't bother me, two hundred seemed like an easy gamble.) Since it was the year of The Gambler, the dealer went with it. Little did he know that I had a queen. I pulled a ten out of the pack and saw his eyes light up with joy, right up until I showed him my queen. I was positively loving this.

I grabbed my backpack and left before he could change the rules on me. Now I was beating them at their own game. This was bringing the race to a whole new level for me.

Ken and PJ pulled off similar creative methods and we all ended up back at the farm an hour later. We found that we had to wait for the rest of the field...for four hours. This gave us four hours of sitting and waiting. We sat and drank a lot of coffee. Organizers were getting soft on us this year or...at least I thought so, right up until the next task.

The Death Race entry process this year required you to have an article in your local newspaper about your participation in the event. The article featuring me focussed on my intent...to WIN the race this year. I knew in my head that I was going to finish or die while trying. Winning was all I was thinking about, to right the wrong I had done the year previous. I had to win in order to know for myself that it wasn't a fluke that I had had a six-hour lead, and it wasn't due to lack of determination, fitness, and skill that I had quit. I had to prove to myself that I was as strong mentally as I knew I should be. As I knew I was.

The next leg of the thirty-hour beatdown involved carrying a rock. A large one. We were told to choose wisely. If organizers deemed the rock not big enough, then they would choose one for us. I was specifically singled out and told that I needed to get a rock that was at least forty percent bigger than anyone else's rock, or they would pick mine. They didn't like the content of my article. Their idea of the event was just to finish. I had enough wits to realize that they were not kidding about my rock choice. In this event nothing is equal between two people, and that's just the way it was going to be. It's never fair. And I love that aspect of it!

How big of a rock did I get? I watched others go through the vetting process and realized that everyone was taking rocks weighing roughly twenty pounds. Some were bigger, and some were smaller. The rocks were not permitted to be carried on our shoulders, nor put in our packs. We had to carry them at our waists the entire time...for eight hours of swamp-donkey hell, through the Bloodroot Trail, in a downpour.

My rock weighed in at forty pounds. It was deemed acceptable. It was brick-shaped and eighteen inches long, and I disappeared with it around the first corner. Out of sight, I dropped it, pulled out my climbing webbing, and built myself a harness to go over my shoulders, wrapping the brick-shaped rock so that it sat nicely at my midline. I could now walk along with my arms free. The weight distributed nicely on my body, and it counterbalanced the fifty pounds of pack on my back. Genius. So much so that Ken and PJ did the exact same thing. Balanced as such, we could almost run, moving as fast as an extra ninety pounds of gear would let us.

We were now thirty-six hours into the event; it was nighttime and pouring rain. We had about 10,000 vertical feet of climbing to do over the next eight hours through the forest, swamp, and bush. Ken, PJ, Amelia Boone, and I all ended up hiking together through the night. Along the way, we picked up Olof Dalner (last year's winner after the Rat Pack quit.) However, he was not happy about having won strictly because we bailed.

While walking in the middle of the night, Amelia suddenly keeled over, landing face first in the mud. At first, I thought she'd had a heart attack, then I realized that she had simply fallen asleep while walking. She had a pulse, and she was just sleeping. I'd heard about this in books but had never seen it in real life. We shook her awake, cleaned her off, and away we went without another word said about it.

It took all of twenty more minutes of trudging through the muck for me to experience the exact same thing. One second I was talking and telling stories, and the next I was struck down by narcolepsy. There I was, face-down in the mud, disoriented, and trying to make sense of what just happened.

Next up was Olof. Instead of sleeping, he began hallucinating and trying to head off to the house he swore he could see to fetch some food. I told him that was where the nasty witch lived, and he should get back on the trail before she threw him in the oven. He thought that was a good idea.

Then I too began to hallucinate. I ran off the trail and told everyone they needed to follow me. I was sure there was a moonlit meadow filled with Dodge Truck hood ornaments for the taking. Again, it was pitch dark, raining, in a forest with no moon. Still, to this day, I can picture those hood ornaments glowing in the field as clearly as the night I saw them, and I'm still pissed that I didn't go pick a few of them. It's amazing what the mind will do to you when you are exhausted, sleep-deprived, hungry, mentally fatigued, and you've pushed the body far beyond anything it is *ever* really meant to do.

The sun's rising the next morning found us at the local reservoir, where we were instructed to enter the freezing water. This explained why we needed to bring a life jacket. A roulette wheel waited to be spun after the first two miles of swimming. The wheel had options for one more mile of swimming, no more swimming, and one black square marked with the requisite threat "Disqualified." While Ken and PJ both got the "no more swimming" option, I managed to get the "swim the extra mile." Ken and PJ took off on the fifteen-mile trek back to the farm, and I took off swimming, shaking and purple from hypothermia.

A long time ago, I was told you can force yourself to warm up by intense concentration and having a burning desire for warmth. Holding fast to this hope, I re-entered the lake. It worked! After a half-mile, I was pink again, happy, and really enjoying my swim. When I stepped out of the water, I was content and relaxed and ready to run like hell to catch up to my buddies, who were now an hour in front of me.

By the time I got back to the farm, it was noon and a scorching 30ºC. Organizers seemed to be conspiring with the weather gods, hitting the extremes. Ken and PJ were just finishing off some log chopping and mudhole diving and were getting ready to head back up the mountain. I was now only a half hour behind them and gaining quickly. Why the hell were they hopping up the road like bunnies, though? I'd soon find out.

With my ankles zip-tied together, I, too, was to bounce up the mountain. I was to familiarize myself with a posted piece of paper on a tree, return, and answer questions about it. The way officials told me to do the task was vital. They distinctly did not say to memorize the contents of what was written; all they said was that they would have questions about it. This could mean anything. I was ready. The hardest part of the task was that if we were to break the zip-ties, we would get a 1000-burpee penalty. I'm pretty sure that even with my love for burpees, 1000 of them would kick my ass. Being the ever-ingenious creative guy, I pulled out some climbing rope and did a much better job of tying my ankles together, ensuring there would be zero chance of me breaking the plastic cuffs.

Heading up the trail, some young kid rocketed past me. I was shocked and in awe. I had never seen that kind of physical intensity displayed before at hour forty of the race. An hour later, I found the kid face down on the ground and delirious. I did a quick head-to-toe and determined that he was suffering from heat stroke and would do fine if he just stayed put. I poured water on him to cool him down and made a mental note to tell the volunteers that there was an injured guy partway up the hill. I decided that he wouldn't die if he was left alone, and there was no need for me to opt out of the race to go get help.

I located the paper-bearing tree 1000 vertical feet later. I memorized everything: the height off the ground, the type of bark, the direction it was facing, and the colour of ink in which it was written.

When I made it back to the bottom, an ambulance had arrived, and attendants were heading up the trail. Apparently, the kid had passed Ken and PJ too. They did the same thing I did. Left him there and sent help when they could.

I was sure the question regarding the paper on the tree was going to be something silly like how many words there were. My instinct was right, because I was asked what colour the push pin was in the top right corner of the paper. Yellow.

I was now only fifteen minutes behind Ken and PJ, and I was gaining fast. Nasty blisters, sore feet, hunger, and hallucinations become much more bearable when you're suffering with others—when you can laugh instead of cry. Being alone in that race was misery at a whole new level.

Tasked with crossing the valley, climbing the newly built stone-slab stairway, and memorizing the details of a cooking stove positioned there before descending to answer questions was the next order of business on the Death Race agenda. I realized I would be coming right back to the same spot, with a two-hour turnaround, roughly, so therefore, I did not require food or water for the trek, as there were creeks everywhere. I ditched my pack behind the farmhouse and took off running, or hobbling, quickly as it felt like the blisters in my feet were going to bore holes through to the bone.

I caught up with Ken and PJ, who gave me shit, chastising me for taking so long to catch up. I soon realized that Olof was only one hour behind us, and we had to gain more of a lead on him before the finish. We really liked Olof and had great respect for him running the World's Toughest Mudder solo, but we still wanted to beat him to show him why we'd had a six-hour lead the year before.

We dug in and began gaining time. Back at the farm, we regurgitated details about the stove: model, make, year, before another ten-mile run to a fitness test, no less.

We had been on course for a little over sixty-three hours. As the sun was going down, the fitness test began. There were ten events to complete, in no particular order.

1. One-mile bear crawl with hands and feet on the ground
2. 500 jumping jacks
3. 10 minutes of plank
4. 4.100 spiderman push-ups, with the added component: as you go down, you bring one knee up to your elbow. 10,000% harder than it sounds.

5. One mile sprint.

6. 200 sit-ups

7. 200 burpees (I actually enjoyed this part)

8. 100 front somersaults. Cue the repeated vomiting.

....and it seems like nobody can remember numbers 9 and 10, but we know we did them.

We all finished the fitness test at the same time. Olof was gaining back on us slightly but remained still roughly an hour behind. Damn, he did well to stay in the game. Being alone in that race is a special kind of loneliness and needed exceptional mental toughness. I guess that was why he ran solo in the World's Toughest Mudder.

I was stunned when we were told to meet back at the big barn at seven the following morning. We would be gambling to get our skulls and were told to bring our tuxedo and all our poker chips from each checkpoint of the race. It was nine p.m., and we had nothing to do until seven a.m. We sat dumbfounded, as we thought this had to be a trick. Were we being set up for failure? I was sure this was just another ruse in the game, so we hung around for another half hour just to make sure we were not being duped.

Apparently, this was it. Our race was done. Currently we had a three-man tie for first.

We went out for dinner and had big ideas on having a huge steak and lots of beer. Sadly, it was hard to force any food in, and I was so exhausted that beer wasn't even sounding good. Sleep was what was needed. In my mind, though, I thought they would have us going out on some new adventure for the first hour of the morning, and that would have been debilitating for sure. After sleep I would be stiff like a board, and in no shape to head back into the hills.

The following morning, dressed in our best, we headed to the barn. The sun was shining, and at least thirty racers were there in their tails, ready to gamble. One at a time, competitors entered the barn, exiting about five minutes later.

Some came out cheering, holding their two-dollar plastic skull that said "Finisher" on it. Others, Ken included, solemnly walked over to their packs, picked them up, and silently walked away across the field and disappeared. We had absolutely no idea what was going on. Now, admittedly, we *were* nervous.

My turn came. I entered the barn. A plastic skull sat at the end of the velvet-covered poker table where a deck of cards was visible. The dealer presided. The building was dark, and a single light was focussed on the table. I was told that we were playing a game of high/low. If I lost, I would lose the skull. I would not be considered a finisher. There would be no first place. Holy shit, this was serious gambling.

I suspected that they might have the deck set to be not in my favour. I split the cards. Both the dealer and I selected cards in different ways to ensure the deck was not rigged.

My jack beat the dealer's ten and I got my skull. Total jubilation and massive relief.

About an hour later, all the racers who had exited quietly came walking back across the field, skulls in hand. It was a setup. They had lost the game of high/low, but had still been granted the skull, regardless. They had been at Joe's house on the other side of the field drinking coffee and eating doughnuts. So well played.

My tuxedo and finisher's skull. One of my prized possessions. Photo: Ken Lubin

I exited the barn celebrating ecstatically, but I had been instructed not to tell anyone what had gone on in the barn and could only tell them that I'd won the skull.

This was the hardest-earned trophy in my life. That two-dollar skull means more to me than anything I've won before.

The race was done. My goal was accomplished. I could now phone home and tell my girls and my wife that I was not a quitter. This I knew for certain. I sincerely apologized for having quit the year before.

I was crying tears of joy and tears of fatigue and pain all at the same time.

I had won.

BAREFOOTING: THE WORLD CHAMPIONSHIPS

MY DESIRE TO COMPETE BAREFOOT WAS STRONG. I WOULD travel all over to competitions. Every tournament featured clinics, so I attended them to immerse myself in learning from a host of barefooters I admired.

I had always had the goal to make the Canadian National Barefoot Water-ski Team. Albeit small, it was still a national team, and in the world of barefooting, being on a national team meant everything. The national team had their names on the backs of their Team Canada suits, and did they ever look cool. I wanted one of those...and I succeeded. This was a big stepping-stone towards attaining my goal.

The first time I went to the World Championships was in 2006. They were held on Lake Silverado in Adna, Washington. I placed ninth overall in the senior men's category.

In 2008, Worlds were held in Otaki, New Zealand. Here, I placed ninth overall again. I did manage to up my stake in the trick event with an eighth-place finish.

My third World Championships, in 2010, were in Brandenburg, Germany.

I will recount some of the lead-up to this event.

My focus remained on training. In addition to barefoot-specific camps, clinics, and coaching, I participated in CrossFit and my first Death Race. All of this enhanced my water-skiing. Now I began to focus on refining and honing a new roster of tricks...

The first was a line-step. Skiing backwards at forty-five mph, I would bend forward, reach between my legs, grab the rope handle, and then pull the rope up between my legs with the handle resting on the inside of my crotch (wearing a jock, of course). In this position, I squeeze the handle with my thighs, tilt a little to the left, and bring my right foot up off the water. Then I repeat with the other foot. This takes a total of one second. Skiing backwards like that, my balance is directly over the middle of my foot, and the heel is only a couple millimetres away from contacting the water. After doing a one-foot with each foot, then I step over the rope and turn around forwards, easy as pie. Or at least it feels like it when it goes right. When executed properly, the effect is spectacular. Disaster strikes if the balance gets over top of the heel, and the heel goes underwater. In this case, the foot gets swept out so fast that there is no time to react, and you're cartwheeling over backwards. The pain is excruciating.

The beauty of this trick combination is that it takes a total of three seconds to do the one- foots and the line step, and it's worth the same points as many people's entire runs. It also has a large potential for failure, which is why not all that many people choose to do it.

The toe-turn was the other big point trick I was working on. This is where I am skiing along on one foot, put my toes into a small pocket built into the handle, and ski along with no hands on the rope. Then, I do a 180° turn on my foot on the water and end up skiing backwards. The crux of the toe-turn is when turning back to the forward position. The toe-back is easy, but the toe-front is kind of the grand poobah of all the barefoot tricks. Failure is common when learning, and success is rare for the first year or more.

The sense of accomplishment upon completing my first toe-front was incredible. The time spent training, trying it, failing it, and getting back up to try it again is hard to quantify. I did spend a lot of fuel and money in the process. By the time I put in trips to Florida, boat gas, coaching fees, and all other costs, I estimate having spent between $40,000–$50,000. I was committed.

Not all barefoot training happens barefoot...especially not when learning these hard tricks.

I practiced using shoe skis. These are basically some "Chuck Taylors" with a stiff rubber pad underneath to increase the surface area so that I can go at a slower speed with less consequence while practicing. Usually, with the shoe skis on I can drop the boat speed down to twenty-eight mph...a totally survivable speed if things go wrong. Then I practice the trick over and over and over until I get to the point where I don't just make the trick, but I can't miss it. Then the transfer to the bare feet at a much higher speed occurs.

Prior to Worlds, there are five days of training available on the competition lake. Usually, each team gets a couple of hours on the water every day, and that time is precious, as it is divided up amongst teammates. This is not the time to be out trying new tricks or changing what you have planned. This is the time to get familiar with the water and the wake. It is also the opportunity to observe exactly what the boat wake does after it hits the shoreline.

In a World Championship event there are two qualifying rounds to make it to the final round. To win the finals, only your score on the last day counts, as the first two rounds are just to get you to the big event. This may or may not mean that you need to pull off your best run in order to qualify. I'd rather just know that I gave it my best every time I was on the water. Knowing in my own head that I did the best is more important to me than anything else—especially if I know I held back and lost.

Round one went well in both the slalom and tricks, and I moved on to the semi-finals. In the jumping event, my traditional style of jumping was surpassed by the guys that do the inverted jumping. I had stopped inverted jumping after getting too many concussions in training.

In the semi-finals, I managed to move on in the tricks, but was not able to make the top eight in the slalom. However, I still was off to the finals on the last day of the competition.

Finals begin with a boat parade. The top eight finalists get in the boat with the flag from their country and do a drive-by in front of the spectator's gallery as the athletes' names are announced. This was my first time doing this, and what an amazing feeling. Years of training, sacrifices, expenses, pain, suffering, and fun were about to be put to the test with fifteen seconds of skiing. On this day, I was ready.

Standing on the start dock with the other top skiers was an incomparable experience. Together, we were one supportive group that wanted everyone to do their best. This remains an odd experience for me—as it is not consistent with the other competitive sports I do—but, at this moment, I was loving the amount of support I was receiving from everyone.

I was skier number three. I had done my dynamic warmups, and my body was fully charged and ready to go. My past sports knowledge fosters this preparatory ability. I was going for one hundred percent effort on this fifteen-second run...and I was going to start it by doing a toe-up.

I gave my start directions to the judges in the boat—with the boat speed I wanted—and what my first trick was going to be. The boat idled away until the rope became taut, and I yelled "Go towboat!" (the starting command). I was in the zone...

The line-step to the front went slow and smooth, and while I was doing it, I heard the voice of Coach in my head saying, *Slow is smooth, and smooth is what makes you fast.* Completing the line step at the start of my run also filled me with a whole new level of confidence, as that really was the key trick in my run with the greatest chance of failure. After it was behind me, the rest of the run went by with little thought at all.

I gave my start instructions to the judges again, readying for pass number two. My breathing was under control, my body felt good, and I knew that the crux on this pass was at the end.

The boat started and I was up skiing backwards and waiting to pass the first couple of rollers before I began my tricks. My focus remained on one trick at a time, and at no point did I let my mind wander to the toe-front that would be at the end of the run. I knew from past experiences that if I let my thoughts get in front of my current trick, then disaster strikes.

My arms were in tight to my body, my foot in the strap felt solid, my core was locked and ready to go, and even my head told me that this was going to go perfectly. The mental part is what's needed the most, because if I don't believe it will work, then how could it?

I made the pivot to the front, and I could see the back of the boat, which was a good sign. I could also feel water washing over the top of my foot, which is a really bad sign. This meant that I had come too far forward and had pushed down on my toes. There is only one thing that happens after this, and you guessed it, I drove into the water going face-first and cartwheeled down the lake like a 747 crashing into the desert.

After I stopped tumbling and came to a rest in the water, I was cheering like a madman. I had just finished my final run at the World Championships, and I'd made every trick in my run that I had. So, while the toe-front would have been the ultimate moment, it was still fine by me that I had crashed. The most important part was that I had gotten to that point and had at least tried. This was more important to me than anything else.

When I got back to the start dock, I got a round of high fives from all the other barefooters. This meant that they also knew this was a damned good run, and to have at least tried the toe-front at the Worlds was a huge accomplishment all on its own. My run was done.

In the other rounds, the boat crew gives a provisional score to the skier for their run, and although it's not an official score, it does give you a good idea of how you did. Not in the finals, though. No information is forthcoming. It's all a guessing game at this point.

Five more skiers to go, and I got to watch and wait. Not knowing the official scores of the other skiers is quite stressful, especially knowing that if there is any question about the score that it will be going to video review.

As the next skiers finished their runs, some had fallen, while others excelled. At this point, I was pretty sure I'd made it to the top three. But the results wouldn't be known for at least an hour or more.

On returning to the viewing area from the start dock, I was greeted by the whole Canadian team, and we were a jubilant bunch. High fives and huge congratulations from the whole team sure made me feel like a hero. A mandate of our Canadian team was that no matter which member of the team was out skiing, all were out on the shore cheering and waving. This kind of support is incredible when you are an athlete...and they were all there.

This is a sport where personal achievement is the biggest reward of all. There is no financial gain for having spent more than $50,000, all told. Nor is there any real funding from the government for being on the National Team. There are few accolades or notoriety, just an immeasurable sense of accomplishment. And that's enough...

Coach came walking towards me. He was holding a piece of paper in his hand and had a blank expression on his face. He stopped in front of me and handed the paper it to me: the results sheet. I began reading at the bottom, scrolling up...

I had won.

By a margin of twenty points, I had become World Champion.

This was just as big of an accomplishment for Coach as it was for me. No athlete, no matter how skilled, in this sport will make it to the top without an incredible trainer and someone who understands how to squeeze the best out of the athlete. Coach had been a pioneering figure in the Canadian barefoot community for years. This was the best possible thing that I could give back as gratitude for his devotion to the sport and his faith in me. I'm forever grateful.

Thanks Richard Gray (Coach), you helped me do the impossible.

LEARNING TO FLY AND PTSD

FOR ME, LEARNING TO FLY A HELICOPTER AND HEALING from PTSD are so intimately intertwined that the two cannot be separated. One only happened because of the other, and they both complement each other.

One of my biggest dreams, since I was a little kid, was to fly. From having dreams where I am flying, to a constant desire to be a pilot, flying has always been something I yearned for. Despite the helicopter crash in 1990, this dream remained. And though I did end up becoming a heli-ski guide, flying every day at work, it wasn't the same as being a pilot.

One day, my extraordinary wife suggested we go to a vision board event. A vision board is a collage of materials that represents goals and hopes, and the event is a night where you learn some things about yourself, distilling what your dreams really are. You take from the evening an understanding of what needs to be done to attain those dreams...and how to get started on making them come to fruition. I made a giant poster with pictures of helicopters, skiers, steaks, BBQs, and all sorts of other things that I desired in my life. There were passages of writing and bold action words on my board as well.

I came home with a rock. On one side of that rock, it said, "My Own Helicopter," and on the other side it said "Plan." I placed it beside my bathroom sink, and there it sat. The poster I'd made hung on the wall of our home gym. Every day I got up, saw the rock on the sink, flipped it over, and read the word "plan," and then I'd put the rock back down. Then when I was in my gym, I'd see the poster with all the motivating sayings, pictures, and dreams that I had pasted on it. The rock and poster stayed there for six months.

I picked up that rock and re-read the four-letter word over and over before I drove to the Heli College of Canada in Langley, British Columbia. At the college, I spoke with the two chief training pilots, Lyle Watts and Geoff Stevens. We discussed flying, buying, and everything else I would need to realize the helicopter dream.

On my drive home I was giddy with excitement. The hardest part of making the dream real was done, as I had signed up for flight school. The course books were on the seat beside me, I was playing music from the *Top Gun* soundtrack, and I was on the road to attaining my dream.

I was to start flight school the following week.

Follow your dreams. Period.

I knew I had married well, because Lee's response was one of encouragement and excitement. The learning-to-fly process was going to take six months. This would have a huge impact on my family because I'd be gone three nights a week in Vancouver for a ground-school course along with the time needed to fly. My family was incredibly supportive, and in turn, I devoted much of my weekends to weekly food preparation for their daily meals.

The one question I received the most was why I wanted to fly. I'd already been in a helicopter crash, and wasn't I pushing it enough just by being a heli-ski guide?

At this point, my dream was more powerfully connected to childhood fantasies than trauma. Or so I thought. This was something I knew I could obtain, and I was going to do it. Choosing to abandon my dream would have been the biggest failure in my life, and that just wasn't going to happen. I wanted to be an upstanding model for my two children. I wanted to lead by example. I'd already shown them that quitting something is the worst-cum-best decision one could ever make, and now I was showing them that following your dream is the most important thing you can do. Without our dreams, what is there to live for? Dreams fuel and fulfil living...and survival.

Many people told me I had done enough in my life already, that I did not need to go prove anything more to myself. I was one of the first snowboarders in the world. I'd survived a helicopter crash. I had won the Death Race. I had been on the podium in the World's Toughest Mudder. I had won the World Championships in barefoot water-skiing. I had become a world-renowned heli-ski guide. Why did I need to do more? Why? Because I could, and because I can. Also, this is not the end of what I am going to do. I've only just begun...I believe I can do anything.

Learning to fly helicopters is a refined process. You are slowly given more and more of the controls as you become a more proficient aviator. The helicopter has four sets of controls to master. Each input you do with one set of controls affects the others. There is the cyclic that rests between your knees, two foot pedals, and a collective on the left with the throttle control on it.

The cyclic controls the left/right and front/back tilt of the aircraft. Push the cyclic to the right, and it adjusts the pitch on the rotor blades, which creates less lift on the right side of the helicopter so that it banks over to the right. A similar process occurs with pushing it to the left, forward, or backward. It takes the next three months of flight school to fully understand the actual mechanics of how this works.

The collective in the left hand makes the helicopter go up and down. Pull up on the collective and it increases the pitch in the rotor blade, which creates more lift, and the houses on the ground get smaller. Push down, and the houses get bigger. Moving the collective also affects torque and spin.

Next, foot pedals come into play. Depressing the left foot pedals will cause the nose of the helicopter to pivot in that direction, and the opposite goes for the right one.

Learning to master all of these at the same time is an incredibly demanding task of infinite multi-tasking. Pull up on the collective, and more left pedal is required. Push down and more right pedal is required.

Flight School: Day One.

I was working on using one control at a time, while hovering five feet above the ground, slowly going up and down the runway. Really, it was a constant battle between me and the instructor. I appeared to be trying to kill us—as often and as fast as possible—and he kept having to take over control of the helicopter, saving our bacon. It was a love-hate relationship between me, the instructor, and the helicopter.

My heart rate was doing about 150 BPM and I was sweating buckets, even though I was just sitting there. Terrified, I constantly over-corrected the machine.

I was terribly stressed and riled up...and following the session, I was not permitted the grace of a beer to help unwind. The best I could muster was an all-cream decaf latté not quite the same.

Beer is not permitted, as alcohol affects the inner ear and balance. Add some ethyl alcohol to the small balance preceptors in the ear, and off goes your balance for the day, as the equilibrium is disturbed. It doesn't do it just on the day you drank the booze, but it lasts for one more day, and sometimes two if you drank a lot. If you want to learn to fly, then out goes the beer, wine, vodka, and rum. Caffeine does a similar thing to your nerves and motor skills. No beer. No coffee. At this point, I was questioning the meaning of life.

Day two went only slightly better than the previous. With my butt cheeks firmly gripping the seat cushion and my hands trying to squeeze the cyclic into mush, I sweated up and down the runway for another hour until my brain was too exhausted to go any longer. At the start, one hour a day was as much as my body could handle, and I was now wondering how many years it was going to take to get the hang of flying. I was not feeling the usual sense of confidence that I normally do when approaching something new. This was disorienting.

I was exhausted.

I was more taxed than when I did the Death Race.

Day three and I was completely spent. I barely had the energy to get into the helicopter.

What was going on?

A friend who was a pilot suggested that I might need to pretend that I was weak with slow reflexes and to stop trying to correct the mistakes I was making. It was, at least, worth a try.

The next flight I went out on, I tried to ignore every instinct that my body had—to just do as little with the cyclic as possible—let all my muscles relax, and fight every desire to correct my mistakes. Total success!

By the end of the third week, I was ready to take on all the controls at the same time. This really was a big deal, because it would mean I would actually be flying the helicopter and not just monkeying with only one or two sets of controls. I thought I was ready for this...but I was wrong.

The part that was so draining about learning to fly was how hard my brain was working to think. No movements felt natural, as I was not flying on instinct. Everything I was doing required intense concentration. The brain happens to burn eighty percent of all our calories in a day. When I ramped up my thought process by 500 percent and my adrenals were pumping full throttle, I burned more calories than if I had just run a marathon.

After finishing that first flight with all the controls, I went over to the grocery store. I bought a whole BBQ chicken, sat down at the curb, and ate the entire thing. I wasn't full. I went back in and bought a rack of ribs and a couple of avocados. This was almost enough. I took myself out for another full-fat-all-cream decaf latté. Now I was content. This confirmed exactly how demanding this learning process really was on me.

As flight school progressed, some things became easier than others. Some things, I was discovering, were damned near impossible. I hate using that word, but that's what was happening to me. I was overwhelmed by doubt.

I could fly up to 800 feet over the ground, roll the engine off, and do an autorotation to the ground with no issue at all. But take-offs and landings confounded me. I'd get down to the point where I was one foot off the ground, and then everything fell apart. The instructor was always forced to take over the controls.

The more I tried, the worse it got. I'd get just above the ground, and my whole body tightened, my feet stopped reacting with the pedals, and I started drifting all over the place. I lost control of my body. This was unfamiliar territory. I am a World Champion. This was pathetic.

The more days I did this, the worse it got. I was beginning to think that maybe, just maybe, the people who had been telling me this was impossible were right. Now I was starting to question whether this was the right dream to be chasing. How the hell was I going to fly solo if I couldn't take off and land? Who would want to fly with me if I seized up every time I got close to the ground? Negative rhetorical questions and doubt began to seep in. This is the exact opposite of what has helped me achieve success throughout my life.

I added more days of flying and more time and more money, and it just was not fixing the problem. I tried meditating and visualizing. I tried sitting in the flight simulator and practicing all the actions so that it would just be muscle memory. I went through the landings and take-offs in my head a thousand times to instill confidence. *Nothing worked.* The only thing I was succeeding with was draining my bank account and creating massive frustration.

Each morning when I walked out to the helicopter, my hands sweated, my heart rate bounded, and I had a sense of absolute dread and anxiety. I did deep-breathing exercises to get my heart rate down, and to try to calm the crazed nervousness that I was experiencing. Nothing helped. If anything, it just made it worse.

I was becoming aware that something else was at play here other than just being nervous about flying.

So, I decided it was time to do a little deep investigation into myself to see if I had more issues than I'd thought.

Twenty-five years before, when I'd been doing my initial recovery from the helicopter crash, two psychologists had told me that

I had post-traumatic stress disorder—or PTSD—and that I would need help to get over it. But I was twenty years old, had just survived a horrendous accident, and considered myself indestructible. I thought the psychologists were out of touch with who I was and what I did, so how could I take their advice? Now, though, I wondered if it was it possible they'd been right. Could I have been hiding my PTSD for the past twenty-five years?

At this point, I was still associating the notion of having PTSD as a weakness. This perceptual hurdle was one that I would have to grapple with, understand, and resolve within my sense of self.

Flight school was shut down for vacation for two weeks.

I had some time to do a little more in-depth analysis. I didn't want to believe that something inside of me was the problem and that I couldn't control it. PTSD was something that combat veterans had from war. How the hell could that be my problem?

I did a lot more reflecting and examined what I had done in my life for recovery after the crash. How did I recover? What things did I do so that I could get back into a helicopter? What did I do to make sure that the effects of the helicopter crash didn't follow me for the rest of my life? What experts did I seek out to find help? Did I really do anything at all, or did I just think I was immune to lingering effects? Maybe, just maybe, I had put up a false front for the past twenty-five years, never directly dealing with the issue. Had I fooled myself? This was becoming a massive string of questions that I didn't have answers for. What I did know was that I had a problem and it needed to be fixed. I just had no idea if it could be fixed or how to do it.

Looking back on what I did to recover from the mental trauma of the crash, I realized it was not much. I had talked with a few counsellors, and they all said I was using my extreme physical output to mask the burden of the emotional trauma I had. It now appeared that they might have been correct.

I looked further into PTSD, researching what it is, how to deal with it, and how to overcome it. But I became more and more disheartened. As far as I could tell, PTSD was not correctable, and it was something I was going to have to live with forever. My research was showing me that the best I could hope for was doing talk therapy for a very long time. In the end it wouldn't get rid of the PTSD, it would just help me control it.

But at this point in my life, I knew there had to be a way around it, even if I hadn't found it yet. I was, however, having to face up to the fact that my fear of flying was connected with PTSD. I was encountering (my own) resistance.

More research. More talking with people that had PTSD. More questions. More belief that there had to be a fix. More frustration. More disappointment. Had I run into a wall I couldn't climb over with brute force and determination?

What I was slowly coming to realize and acknowledge was that over the past twenty-five years, I had taught myself ways to cope with PTSD—ironically by denying it.

Now, some two-and-half decades after the accident, my PTSD was (re)surfacing in take-offs and landings. I was not blind to the implicit significance of the metaphor.

So...where did this leave me? I was feeling screwed...and then it happened...

I ran into a friend, and there was life showing me the answer.

In conversation, he mentioned that he had gotten rid of his ADD at fifty years old. He had been seeing a psychologist in Whistler. PTSD bears many similarities to ADD. They are both involuntary responses from the brain. Needless to say, I sat there and talked with him for the next hour and learned everything I could about what he had done.

I learned he'd gone through a low-energy neurofeedback system, or LENS for short. I walked away with the phone number for Dr. Stephen Milstein at the Mountain Psychology Clinic. Right in Whistler, where I lived! I phoned Dr. Milstein first thing in the morning.

Dr. Milstein wanted to know why I thought I had PTSD. I told him about the accident. After I'd talked for about five minutes, he told me to stop because he had all the information he needed. How could he have all the info he needed, as I had barely told him anything about the crash and hadn't yet talked about learning to fly? From his side of the table, it was very obvious that I had PTSD, and there was no reason to sit there talking about the accident, as it wouldn't help a thing. What he was saying was the exact opposite of everything the world had told me about post-traumatic stress disorder.

But I did tell him I was a heli-ski guide and that I flew around in helicopters all day long. I told him I liked helicopters so much that I was in flight school, and I was going to get my own helicopter. I also told him about the problems I was encountering with flight.

I've learned an incredible amount about PTSD from what may cause it, to how we cover it up, and now all about how to get rid of it. This was no longer something I would have to live with for the rest of my life. The relief was indescribable.

Post-traumatic stress disorder is a condition in which the body has an adverse, involuntary response to a sight, sound, smell, memory, situation, or external stimuli. The person with PTSD does not get to choose what the adverse response is, or how and when it will manifest. What is traumatic to me, may not be traumatic to you. We don't get to choose what our brain deems as traumatic, but we do have some control over whether or not that trauma lingers to cause issues later in life.

To better understand how trauma remains with us, we need to understand how REM sleep works. REM stands for Rapid Eye Movement. At night, when we go into a deep sleep mode, we go through REM sleep. If you were to observe someone sleeping, you would notice their eyes twitching quickly from side to side. This is understood to be the brain processing the day's events, assimilating the information, which in turn allows the brain to move on to the next day without any lingering effects from the previous day's events.

There are many things that will interfere with REM sleep. Drugs and alcohol are two of the major contributors to the problem, and most of society turns to exactly those two items when they require emotional support. Drugs and alcohol will suppress your normal sleep rhythms, creating a new problem. Pain medication for an injury can have the same effect.

Society supports talking about these things to help get over them, not to bottle them up inside. Sadly, this is exactly the worst possible thing you could do if you've just had a traumatic event, compounded with not sleeping well. By talking about it, you are reliving the event. For your brain, this is like being in the accident all over again. And if your brain is not given a chance to process the event at night through REM sleep, the trauma becomes further embedded. The body starts to develop ways of protecting itself from the anxieties that start to show up. This is referred to as disassociation.

When I was in the hospital after the helicopter crash, the psychologists who came to help me only dealt with my denial that I was going to lose my ear and nose. Nothing else was offered relating to the rest of the trauma that I had been through. Upon my release from the hospital, a physiotherapist I was seeing suggested I attend a burn-counselling meeting. I did go and check it out.

At that meeting, the burn survivors were only discussing how much pain they were in and how hard their road ahead was going to be. As I looked around the room to assess what kind of burns and other trauma these people may have had, I couldn't see anything. No visible scars. No visible burn garments, and certainly nobody with a horribly disfigured face who was wearing a plastic mask.

This mindset was exactly opposite of what I was looking for. I was in a room full of people who were not on a road to recovery. This group of survivors was going down a deep, dark hole as fast as possible, and nobody was pulling the emergency brake. If I stayed around them any longer, they were going to suck me into their black hole too. As I sat in on that meeting, it felt to me that this was the saddest experience I'd ever encountered. I was twenty years old, one of the top snowboarders in the world, and very eager to get back on snow as fast as possible. I was highly motivated, to say the least.

I got up and left halfway through.

On reflection, this may have been one of the better times in life for me to step up and see what good I could do. That group of survivors needed a person to link on to for positive influence, and I had walked out the door. I was motivated when I was twenty years old, but I had yet to develop compassion for others. Not until years later, when I connected with the Burn Fund in Vancouver, did I get a better understanding of the recovery process burn survivors need. I needed to apologize to the folks in that original meeting for my rude and inconsiderate behaviour. I only wish I had the chance.

For me, though, that was it. Emotional support had just ended. One cannot be helped until he or she is ready. At twenty years old, I was not ready.

For the next twenty-five years, my emotional coping mechanism became a life of pursuing extreme sport.

When we go through a traumatic event—or any event, for that matter—we create a memory. These memories can be recalled at any time. They may be very intense, instill joy or fear, and some can even trigger our sense of smell and taste. At times, the body may be overwhelmed by our memory-response.

Following the helicopter crash, I quickly learned how to relay the story of what had happened, and about the people who'd died, and how I escaped, without it becoming emotional. Little did I know I was just making things worse. I was imbedding the trauma even deeper.

I protected myself by only telling the story of the accident from a third-person point of view. I explained things from a different perspective. I told the story from the viewpoint of a camera hovering above the scene. I could talk about it without reliving the event because it was not happening to me. I had disassociated myself from the event so that it was just a story. I had to tell the experience like this, otherwise I'd break down in tears as I relived the horror of being burned alive inside a flaming tin can.

This third-person narrative is what enabled me to function for twenty-five years without having to face up to what had happened. I was burned to the point where it was a wonder that I was alive. I'd lost three good friends that were sitting beside me. And now I had a lifetime of living with horrific facial scarring and associated trauma. I needed defenses to allow me to function in my everyday life.

In the process of creating these mental defenses, the brain had created shortcuts in its normal memory process; the electrical patterns had become unbalanced. It's like the brain had installed its own programming to circumvent the memory allocation.

I really wish PTSD was not referred to as a disorder, as it's not. What it really is, is an unhealed injury.

Using LENS, the first thing that happens is that a map of the brain's electrical activity is created. Twenty-one electrodes are attached to your scalp, and a computer program analyzes the brain's activity over several sessions. Based on what is found, the task then becomes to help the brain reset all of the errant electrical pathways so that they go back to where they were before the trauma.

LENS is considered a disruptive technology. The process is surprisingly quick, requires no input from the patient, and can help treat a myriad of different conditions and problems.

I was able to get in three sessions with Dr. Milstein in the following two weeks. I was not sure of the effectiveness of the treatment, as I did not really feel a large difference. Maybe there was less anxiety towards thinking of flying? I was not sure.

It was time to return to flight school.

I approached the machine.

I wasn't sweating. My heart rate was normal. I felt like Luke Skywalker now.

It had only been two weeks.

I calmly looked my instructor in the eye and said, "Today it's different." I then proceeded to lift off into a perfect hover. And then land it without incident.

After my fourth session with Dr. Milstein, he asked if I liked doing crosswords. I said no, I hated the things. I always knew I should know the word, and after looking at the answers I knew I should have known it, but I did not. I was sure I was a smart human, but even the simplest crossword would confound me.

Home I went, and out came the crosswords. I finished the first one in about thirty minutes, and moved onto the second, the third, and the fourth. I do not know what had shifted, but suddenly I had become a freaking word sleuth. This really was like being handed a miracle.

On my return to the doctor's office, he showed me the before and after pictures of the electrical activity in my brain. The images were revelatory. They showed me the drastic changes in where the electrical activity had now been equalized between the two sides of my brain. The reason for the ability to do crosswords was related to balancing the portion of the brain responsible for memory and word recall.

Dr. Milstein said he had one more thing that would help process the traumatic events in my head and allow me to change the perspective of my memories. This would involve the use of Eye Movement Desensitization and Reprocessing, or EMDR. It employs the same methods that REM sleep does to process your day's events in your mind.

EMDR involves tracking a light moving across a bar from side to side with just your eyes. This would be simulating the REM eye movement. While moving my eyes, I went back into my own memories to go through the helicopter crash events again. Dr Milstein told me to just accept where my thought process went, and not to judge myself for any of the thoughts that may come into my mind.

As I went through my memories of the crash and what it was like to be inside the raging inferno, my body let loose everything that had been pent up for the past twenty-five years. Emotions flooded out of me in surges. Tears streamed down my face as I shook and sobbed uncontrollably, yet at the same time, I could not take my eyes off the moving light bar that was instigating this. I genuinely thought I was in the process of a total meltdown and was terrified and delighted at the same time.

I was a sweating mess and I smelled horrid. Toxic build-up was leaching out of my skin. My memories raced through the crash and bounced around to numerous other moments in my life that held smaller traumas as well. I was shocked at some of the memories that surfaced and how powerful they felt. I really started to wonder if I was more messed up than I thought.

Following the EMDR sessions, and for the first time in twenty-five years, I was remembering the event through my own eyes! I was no longer telling or remembering the story from a third-person point of view. The associated trauma connected to the event was gone, and my brain no longer needed to try and protect me from it. The memory wasn't gone, and it hadn't changed, it was just the perspective from which I was able to approach it that had adjusted. I was finally cured of the PTSD and its associated hold on my body.

A person can no more just "get over" their traumatic response any more than a person can just "get over" their broken leg. At least they can't get over it until the original injury is healed. Sadly, the support and healing that is provided in society right now shames anyone with PTSD, anxiety, and a myriad of issues with regards to mental trauma. It is changing, but quite slowly. We are collectively overcoming the stigma and misunderstandings surrounding mental health, which may have labelled people as weak, liars, hypocrites, or failures.

Slowly though, attitudes are shifting. We need to learn vitally new ways to offer support and to allow ourselves to be supported.

I consider myself to be one of the mentally strongest people on the planet, and it took me twenty-five years to be ready to listen to the information that I'd been given all those years ago. Joke was on me. I'm exceptionally happy to be where I am now, but I only wish I had been a better listener when I was told I had a problem.

As I thought back on the changes in my life since the helicopter crash, I realized that the LENS fixed a lot more issues than just the PTSD with my flying. When I was a young kid snowboarding, I really thought of myself as fearless. I had no issue with trying ridiculous new tricks and landing on my head or jumping off a forty-foot cliff and landing in tight trees in the forest. Fear of heights? What was that? Well, that was all before the crash.

Afterwards, though, my life was a different story. Until the PTSD was gone, I never realized how many other aspects of my life it had been affecting.

For the previous twenty-five years I'd had a fear of heights, and I didn't even know how it had crept into my life. I had never had this issue before and was quite shocked one day to find how much it was controlling me. It became my new normal. I didn't know how miserable that had become until I found that it was gone. The fear of heights went away with the PTSD. This was going to be an epic piece of my life going forward.

With my PTSD eradicated, I was ready to resume my flight training. School proceeded quite quickly and smoothly after that. I finished with a commercial pilot's license in my hand, staring at my own helicopter. The dream had come true.

Yes...my own helicopter. I left out the part in the middle of this story where I ended up buying my own helicopter.

When I'd started flight school, I told the instructors that I would finish the last half of flight school in my own helicopter. They took me at face value. Apparently, this is quite common.

I located a used one in Calgary, negotiated the deal, and asked Lyle if he would come to Calgary with me and help fly it back. This ended up being one of the greatest flights through the Rocky Mountains ever. Clear blue sky, no wind, no traffic, and nothing but the most scenic day of my life.

Picking up my helicopter in Calgary with my mom.

I'd grown up around the Rockies, hiking with my family every weekend, snowboarding, and skiing, and I had driven the highway hundreds of times. From above, I became a mountain tour guide for the day, sitting content in the realization of my dream.

From where my headspace had been during the initial phase of flight school to where I was now, piloting my own machine, felt quite surreal. Flying solo might just be one of the greatest freedoms I've ever had. This was most certainly the capstone of dream-chasing for me.

WHO ARE WE WITHOUT SPORTS?

WHAT HAPPENS TO A PROFESSIONAL ATHLETE WHO CAN NO longer compete in the sport (or sports) that has made them a living? This is a monumental question. The answer remains complex...

During my years of professional athletics, I encountered almost every injury a person could sustain, just shy of losing a limb. I broke a leg. Both wrists. Two elbows. I had my ACL replaced, along with my hamstring tendon. A chunk of bone fell out of my ankle and locked it up so much that it needed surgery. I shattered my nose and sustained massive facial burns. I dislocated both shoulders, multiple times. As well, I have had numerous untreated concussions. Add to that list every possible strain and muscle tear imaginable.

Any one of these injuries could have taken me out of contention for any future sport endeavors. Some would say I was lucky none of these injuries kept me away from sport permanently. I say luck had nothing to do with it. Dogged determination and a burning desire to never accept no as an answer is what kept me returning to the sports I love. Being motivated by a refusal to give up enabled me to constantly return. This was the opposite of luck. Every injury forced me to consider who I would be if I could not return to my sporting life. Each time I was in the emergency room, I wondered if this was the end of doing what I loved. Doing what I love required huge effort in the recovery aspect of sport, though.

Looking back, I would say that the level of devotion I put into my sports was more than likely due to the PTSD. The sports that I put all my life force into were just a means to escape. They became my coping mechanisms— I was self-medicating with the physical exertion to avoid dealing with the mental anguish from the helicopter crash. I'm sure I still have a piece of paper that was written by a psychologist from 1991 that says the exact same thing. Sometimes I think that I should be more thankful for the PTSD, as without it I may not have done all the things I did. That is a bit of a slippery slope of thought process to go down, though, and I try not to dwell on all those things for too long,

I certainly know that since I vanquished the PTSD, my desire for the intense, body-destroying sports has waned. I have come to realize that my family needs me in one piece more than I need to prove to myself that I can do the impossible in sports one more time. I did just finish my fastest ten-kilometre running race at fifty-one years old, though. Maybe some things never change.

After being on the podium of the World's Toughest Mudder, it took my body three months to rebound back to the point that I could go to the gym again. My entire metabolic system had turned off. Everything that was me was gone. I was not an athlete. I could not run. I was not able to lift weights. I was even wondering if I would be able to ski the following winter. Without those things, who was I? This was a terrifying place to be in life.

The healing took time.

Since I do still get out mountain biking in the summer, skiing in the winter, flying helicopters, and water-skiing, I must have finally figured this all out. Well, sort of. Not quite. It's still a work in progress. What I have done is taken my own advice. Instead of trying to make the giant leaps ahead, I have begun approaching life one small step at a time. This now means that instead of trying to set a record for the ten-kilometre race, for example, I just try to run it a little bit faster each year. Even if it was only two seconds faster, then that is now acceptable to me. Baby steps refreshingly: healing, supportive, and nutritive.

I have reflected on all aspects of my life and discovered that beyond high-performance athletics, I really do enjoy the teaching aspect of sports. So, I have begun further emphasizing that.

Once I discovered the Vancouver Fire Fighters Burn Fund, I was introduced to motivational speaking and helping others to get through PTSD. Since then, I've assisted in helping at least seventy friends go through the LENS program to confront their own trauma. I really had no idea that so many people I knew had similarly been suffering. This was a serious eye opener in life, one that has bred my compassion and empathy.

Lastly, my search for more of who I am led me to writing this book. Helping others get through their challenges in life is what I am finding to be my new purpose. Hopefully you can learn from many of the experiences that I went through and the methods I used to recover. Learning from others is vital, as we certainly don't have enough time in life to make all the mistakes ourselves.

DISCOVERING ALTERNATE HEALING

EVERYONE HAS THE POWER TO HEAL AND BE WELL. IN OUR Western culture, however, it is easy to become complacent or to be swayed by the tremendous influence of the mainstream food industry and the power of multinational pharmaceutical companies and an allopathic health system that treats symptoms, not root causes. Intuition and decades of traditional—now, alternative—methods of healing have gotten suppressed by the capitalist structure.

The human body is an amazing piece of machinery. We can beat it up, smash it, break it, bend it, over-use it, under-use it, poison it, and ignore it, and for some reason it tries to find ways of bouncing back and moving forward. Right up until the time that it doesn't.

When faced with adversity, many people place all their chips on their doctor and, possibly, a host of drugs to keep them alive and well. There is a time and place for everything. I am not going to deny for a moment that I haven't benefitted from exceptional help from our traditional medical system. I am alive to this day because of it. What I am saying, however, is that alternative strategies and approaches do exist—some with long, practiced lineages, others harnessing modern technology. It often may not be a case of "either/or"; rather, it might be a supportive "both." I tend to turn towards non-standardized practices first, whilst not denying the offerings of our current overarching system. In my experience, though, often the mainstream medical world has a hard time looking outside the box to find the answers.

My seventy-year-old mother-in-law, Donna, was one of the best examples ever to show me a never-ending search for health and how powerful it could be. She had twelve bladder infections in a year, and our modern system was failing her badly with antibiotics and possible surgery. In the end, the answer was to stop eating sugar and take a mild yeast killer. This protocol was found through a naturopath in Vancouver.

Donna was then diagnosed with terminal cancer and given a prognosis of only a few months to live. She tried everything from chemotherapy to Chinese herbal therapy, to hemp oils, and everything in between. Her words were: "In the end, I will not know what worked, but I do not have time to wait on just one cure. I will try them all!" She lived for another seven years and taught me that I do not want to be as tough as nails, I want to be as tough as an old lady. She had a will to live that was more powerful than any medicine on the planet.

After witnessing the cure for Donna being the elimination of sugar, Lee and I went home and proceeded to throw out all the sugar in the house and make a dramatic change in our diet. We decided that we didn't need to wait another thirty years for a doctor to tell us we had limited time to live. We would make that change now, as the answer had already been given to us, and luckily, we had been listening.

Over the past thirty years, I have discovered my own way through injury, rehabilitation, exercise, naturopaths, and diet, and from having several doctors suggest operations to fix things that didn't need fixing. I have had to become my own health advocate.

One of the most powerful healing abilities of all is harnessing the power of our minds and mental attitudes. Healing does not happen when anger, frustration, and doubt are front and centre in the thought process. One requires a positive outlook above all else. Believing that you will heal is the priority. Having a focus on exactly what you want is mandatory. The body will follow along with what your brain is thinking.

Attitude is everything, and that is a choice that only you get to make.

Our bodies have evolved over millions of years to move, hunt, and gather food. They are supposed to be using all the different muscle groups each day so that the whole system stays in balance. The body was not designed to sit at a desk or watch TV for five hours a day while the abs shorten, the hip flexors tighten, and the back hunches. Inactivity is one of the greatest poisons to the human body, but it is what most people live their lives by, every day.

Everybody gets to where they are in life by making choices. We just may need support in choosing paths that best serve to foster and fuel our systems, rather than voiding the warranty if we had one. It must be mentioned that levels of privilege, socio-economic status, and education greatly factor into people's ability to access various levels of support. It comes down to trying to do the best within your means. This is going to mean, and be, something different for every individual body. I like the infinite wisdom of Yoda: "Try you must."

Recovering from my burns, I discovered meditation. Following the smashing of my elbows and luxury bone removal with the chronic pain, I discovered acupuncture and Rolfing. Both are powerful and recommended healing modalities. I have continued through the years to add other supportive strategies and frameworks to my healing regimen. Exercise and nutrition have always been key. So too, has the use of the Bemer machine, fasting, and cleanses as well as traditional Chinese medicine, blood analysis, infrared therapy, LENS, and EMDR.

Valid evidence is a nice thing in life, as is knowing that the path you are going down is the right one for you. Some evidence only comes from lived experience.

Through the Death Race and with the CrossFit gym, I rearranged my nutritional intake and switched to a mix of ketogenic and Paleolithic eating. While it is not for everyone, it certainly was a key element for me. I really believe my success in the Death Race was due more to nutrition than anything else.

Not everything works for everybody, but if you don't at least try, then that means you are accepting failure. I don't do well with failure. And when you decide that success is the only option, failure will never enter the picture. For me, this has always meant seeking alternatives. I support you in your journey to do the same.

LIFE LESSONS LEARNED

WHILE I WAS IN THE BURN UNIT, MOM GAVE ME A BOOK written by a plane crash survivor. It was a fascinating story about what had happened, what kind of burns he had, and how he had survived the plane crash in the woods. Then I got to the part where he was describing his time in the burn unit and how he treated the nurses, his family, and those around him as well as the horrific rut that he got himself into mentally. I read one more chapter about what a miserable person he was and how poorly he treated everyone who was trying to help him. It created such a strong emotional response in me that I gave the book back to my mom and just said thanks. I hated pretty much everything about who he was, how he was dealing with his situation, and his own dislike of himself. This was everything that was not me.

Although I never finished that book, it was one of the more motivational reads I had ever come across. It triggered a strong response inside of me and helped form who I am. I knew that I would never treat those who were helping me like that, ever. I would be thankful for the help I received, and I would make sure I was always in a positive state of mind to help with my recovery.

Mostly, life has taught me that when someone tells me something is impossible, that it is only their opinion. I am the only one who gets to decide if it is impossible for me or not. I've often said that people refer to a thing as impossible only because nobody has done it yet. Would you have thought that a car would be sent into space by a millionaire fifty years ago? Probably not.

One week after elbow surgery and wearing the mask.
I was always upbeat with a smile on my face.

Now, at the end of *this* book, I find myself wanting to leave the reader with a distilled list of my take-aways, of my lessons learned—be they through injury, infatuation, imagination, or inspiration...what they all hold are the possibilities held within the impossible:

- A positive attitude is everything.
- No matter how hard you think your situation is, someone else has been through worse and is still here.
- Healing is my choice. Nobody else will do it for me.
- To succeed, I need to have a specific goal and a burning desire to achieve it.
- Quitting is not an option for me.
- Anything is possible; I am the only one who sets limits on myself. I must believe I have the ability to do it.
- Getting back up is more important than how hard I got knocked down.
- Keep an open mind.

My race with death ran me into a life full of living...

ACKNOWLEGEMENTS

THE JOURNEY OF WRITING THIS BOOK WOULD NOT HAVE been possible without an incredible amount of help, support, and encouragement from a plethora of friends and family. Upon commencing this project, I realized that I was a great athlete, but not much of a writer, and was going to have to tackle another impossible task.

As usual in my life, what I needed showed up the next day. I was talking with my daughter's ski instructor who said he was writing a book of his own, and he passed along the info of a person who specializes in getting people on track for their books. Mike Skrypnek was this person and he convinced me that this book was not only possible but would turn out to be an epic tale. The best thing he said was to just start writing and see where the ideas fell. I sat down that night and put fingers to the keyboard. Mike's advice was monumental in the start of the book as I quickly found that putting the ideas to paper was easier than I would have thought.

After I had decided that I was going to attack this task, it came to light that I knew little about writing, and even less about how to go about putting all my life's events into a coherent and logical story. For this bit of wisdom, I first asked my daughter, Lydia. She works weekly with a creative writing coach and is currently working on her own book, so she seemed like a good place to start. I phoned Bronwyn Preece, and we talked for an hour about the idea, the project and what it would take to get my writing edited to a level that would be suitable for print. Bronwyn was a monumental motivator and a constant inspiration to my writing.

The hit to my ego was the most challenging aspect of writing. I would send Bronwyn one hundred and twenty pages of writing, and she would hand me back forty pages after editing. This took a bit to get used to, but she constantly assured me that the extra eighty pages, although entertaining, did not add to the story and message that I wanted to convey. In the end, Bronwyn was the key element in making this a book of two hundred and fifty pages of solid entertainment, and not one thousand pages of poorly written dribble.

I also need to thank my wife Lee, who spent countless days pouring over the manuscript and constantly correcting me on my usage of grammar, run on sentences, and misusage of first and second-person prose.

Dr. Georgann Watson was crucial in how I presented my ideas. Her honesty and assistance in how to write without insulting or belittling my readers was monumental. It was at Georgann's birthday dinner that Lee and I had our first date and our first kiss. I owe her many thanks.

In the process of creating this book, I discovered FriesenPress, and decided that if I wanted to get this book on the shelf ASAP, then the self-publishing route was probably my best option. They have been an invaluable aid in the creation of the book and have incredible staff that have kept me pointed in the right direction through this journey. Many thanks go out to Rhonda at FriesenPress for her editing skills and pushing me to take the book from average to epic. She handed me back an edited book and said "I need 20,000 more words please. I need you to tell more of your stories." This was what finally filled me in on what I knew the book needed. More entertaining stories and journeys of hilarity that I've lived through.

My longtime friend, Bob Jaffee of Jaffe Films read my first draft and told me it needed more. He didn't say what "more" was, or how to achieve the "more", but those were certainly the words I needed. I understood what he meant. Thanks, Bob, for your many hours of phone calls and honesty.

Thanks to my brother who likes to read all the same books that I do and was honest enough to read the first draft and say to me that it was a 70% book. He wasn't sure what was missing, but it needed to be at least 90% to be awesome. This was exactly the kind of thing that works for me.

Most of all, I need to thank the rest of my friends who told me they were eagerly awaiting the release of my book, and how excited they were to read it. This constant belief in me from them kept me writing long after I thought it the book was done.

If I forgot to thank you, then I'm sure I'll make up for it in my next book. I have no idea what that one will be about, but there is so much fun content on the editing room floor, that there is room for two more books for sure.

CPSIA information can be obtained
at www.ICGtesting.com
Printed in the USA
BVHW040826240523
664743BV00004B/17

9 781039 135727